www.janedienomore.org

BURYING JANE DOE

A Journey of Courage and Strength

To Carrie

May you realize your
purpose & be the blessing
you want to be to others!

Love you!

Barb

Barb Jenkins *Jenkins*

Jer 29:11

ISBN 978-1-64003-453-2 (Paperback)
ISBN 978-1-64003-454-9 (Digital)

Covenant Books, Inc.
11661 Hwy 707
Murrells Inlet, SC 29576
www.covenantbooks.com

CONTENTS

FOREWORD

———◆◆———

Barb Boucher Jenkins came into my life in the fifth grade. I have known her in many phases of our lives. We have been there for each other through life's celebrations and traumas, happy times and despair; and our friendship has remained strong. She has been through so many trials in her life from child abuse, to moving place to place, to multiple miscarriages, to rape. One person can only take so much, and yet she gave herself to God to guide her and give her strength and peace with each situation. She is kind and loving and gives everyone the benefit of doubt as a child of God.

She has always been my connection to God and prayed for me when I needed her prayers, sometimes calling me to find out what was bothering with me, as we had that connection of just knowing when we needed each other. She found a wonderful loving husband, Al, and has two beautiful children, Ethan and Grace. They are her light and love, and she would do anything for them.

Barb has put herself out in the community to help others in need, whether through the church or creating her own benefits to help others. She has had dinners for soldiers to honor them. She has gathered warm blankets and socks to keep the homeless warm in the winter and helped with any cause that pulls at her heart. I know she will continue to shine her light on people no matter where she goes or no matter what happens to her. God has made her that strong. If she loves you, she loves you fiercely! We are all better people by just knowing her.

I invite you to read this book and see the struggles and heart-aches of one woman. Rape affects so many people, not just the victim. It is becoming too common in our society and just dismissed in many cases. Finding peace and self-worth is the struggle for many who have had similar trauma in their lives; you will find healing and *love* again. God's love is really the answer.

—Leah Pankratz Heilman

INTRODUCTION

Not everyone will understand your journey. That's fine.
It's not their journey to make sense of. It's yours.

An excerpt from my victim impact statement:
To Your Honor,

If I may, I have prepared a statement to Johnathan and will include it here:

Hello, My Name Is Jane Doe

You stole my identity. You stole my peace. You opened the floodgates of my eyes and burst the dam. You tried to crush my spirit. You stole what wasn't yours to take. You disregarded me as a human being. You closed your ears to my pleas. You repaid my selflessness with your selfishness. You mocked me for my faith. You drug my name through the mud and slung dirt at my face. All the while pretending you didn't do this. I have wondered over and over again, "How? Why?" How could you, the person I freely gave my friendship to, turn around and rape me? Don't sit there and pretend you don't know right from wrong. How dare you play the part of the confused innocent man! You know what you did and you know you planned it. And you also know I know that about you too. You sized me up that day. You squeezed my injured foot and saw how much pain that caused me.

You knew I was serious when I told you I would never come back to McCormick Park again since you were obviously living there again.

You hurt my body. Yes, it took a couple of days for the full impact to hit me, but I assure you it did. You hurt my soul. You carelessly did what you did and then simply stepped back and put your hands down at your sides and looked at me with no expression. How black your soul must be to do that to the one person who believed in you and your potential. My body has healed from what you did that day. No more bruises and no more abrasions exist on my private parts. But the effects linger. The stress you have caused me has reared its ugly head in many ways. I am now 30+ pounds heavier. The stress hormone is present on my midsection like a lingering hangover. My digestive track is all messed up. I have heartburn like never before, my migraines last for weeks at a time, I am nauseous more often than not, I have body tremors and the fibromyalgia I have suffered with for years is now completely off the charts. I wake up each morning to a body that screams in agony. My every joint aches. My legs cramp and my shoulders throb from tension. I have no balance in my body anymore. It will take me months if not years to regain what you stole from me.

Nights are the worst for me. I don't sleep uninterrupted anymore. I wake up at 2:30, 3:30, 4:30, 5:30 and rarely sleep a whole night through, even with the aid of melatonin. I wake from nightmares and find myself in terror because I can't get myself regulated back to reality. My nightmares consist of you and that day. I feel your breath on my face, I feel the impact of your methodical and hard thrusting on me, I feel the sickness of the release you had on me, I smell your stench and I feel the total lack of my ability to do anything to stop you. I see the three people on the walking path walking by and I call out to them in my mind and yet they keep on moving.

When I look in the mirror I wonder who that is looking back at me. Because, I don't recognize that woman. She has a haunted expression in those eyes. You dimmed the brightness she once had in her eyes. She doesn't smile and laugh freely anymore. She is guarded and has deep sadness in her heart. She is a shadow of someone I once knew. Do you remember that person? I do. She was happy and bubbly and loving. She was full of kindness and compassion. She always gave the benefit of the doubt to everyone. She gave of herself freely and unreserved. That's what others say she was like. Not so anymore, thanks to you. How's your tummy feeling right now, Johnathan?

Jane exists because you stole my name. She is a faceless woman who lives with deep pain. She lost her song for weeks, not daring to utter anything but sobs. Hello, I am Jane Doe. I spent the first 3 months crying so much that the skin under my eyes was raw. I never used to have bags under my eyes, but I sure do now. I struggled every day just to get out of bed and go through each day as if nothing had happened. I despised each breath I took because that meant I was still here to live with the memories of what you did to me that day. I hold my breath when I cross over Orange Street Bridge. I don't dare to look in the direction of McCormick Park. I panic when I see a man in a red coat; even more so when they have long hair or a beard.

When I smell body odor it causes me to relive your nasty stench. The sensory overload is more than I can handle. My heart beats erratically, my palms sweat, my brain goes numb, my breathing is shallow, my legs go weak and I shake. I have to focus really hard and pep talk myself that I am ok and it isn't happening again, right here and right now.

You stole my security. You stole my freedom. The things I once enjoyed are now a distant memory. I'm too full of anxiety to go out alone and walk or run. I don't even go to a park alone anymore to have my lunch. If I do go to a park, I sit inside my car with the windows up and the doors locked. On occasion if I get the courage to venture out of my car, my new best friend Mace is right there with me holding my hand. I can't relax. My body and mind are at full alert and I am extremely jumpy.

For 11 months, my "normal" was a big black cloud of uncertainty hanging over my head and the heads of my husband, son and daughter. How awful it is to know that as your victim I was going to be re-victimized by the system that was supposed to protect me from you, but instead protected you! Was it not enough to be violated by you on that day that you needed to put me and my family through more? You didn't even have the moral fiber in you to stand up like a man and admit what you did to me. Again, I have asked over and over, "Why? How?" Now I will ask you again, how does your tummy feel Johnathan? Where is your shock? Where is your remorse? Where is an inkling of sorrow for what you have done to me? Do you remember me now? Who am I? I am taking me back from you. You don't get to have that control and power over me anymore. I am picking up the shattered pieces of me and I am being glued back together again. And that light in my eyes that you attempted to block out with your hand? It's coming back. And it is brighter than ever. Why? Because I know the one who put that light there and he has never left me for a second. You will never be able to extinguish it. Was the light in me too bright for your darkness? Is that why you covered my eyes?

Today, Jane Doe will take her rest. She has served me well. She has protected me and given me time to face you. She has given me strength to be me. And I am proud to be me, despite what you did to me. This is your shame, not mine. Your actions have held me hostage for a long time. My hatred of you for what you did to me has held me hostage for a long time. But you don't get the luxury of that control any longer. I am releasing the anger and releasing the hatred and replacing it with things that have zero to do with you and your existence. Forgiveness is something I am working on. It is a choice I need to make every day of my life. I never thought you would hear the words "I forgive you" coming from me, but I do forgive you Johnathan. Not for your benefit, but mine.

My faith dictates to me that I need to forgive you and because I do love God from the bottom of my heart, I will forgive you. I pray for this ability constantly and I even pray for you to be forgiven by God himself, but that is totally in your control, not mine. You are the one who needs to make that step toward him. Not me. My forgiveness to you, however, does not give you permission to vandalize my life in any way at any time and it does not release you of the reality of what you carried out on me. It simply sets me free. Free from anger and bitterness so I can continue to heal and become a better me.

Your new reality will soon begin. I hope you spend every single moment of your existence remembering the choices you made and I hope they are the cause of your own sleepless nights. I wish they would lock you up for the rest of your life and throw away the key. At least there you can't hurt me or anyone else again. And maybe, just maybe, you might finally get the help you need. You can't make it up to me and my family by saying you are sorry. You can't undo what you've done to me. You can't erase my nightmares and flashbacks. You can't make me who I once was. You have in effect given me a life sentence. I will live with the memories of your actions until the day I die. But my life will never be the unproductive excuse that you have chosen. And you did choose your path Johnathan. You have pushed away all who love you and tried to help you and you threw your life away by your own choice. Your mental illness is only a crutch for bad choices and immoral behavior. Denial is a one-way river and you hold the paddles. You still possess the ability to know right from wrong and to choose one or the other. You and I both know that. My life will be full and rich in spite of you. Because mine is full of love and goodness and grace and mercy. I will take this experience and learn from it and I will help others so they don't suffer as I have.

Hello. My name is no longer Jane Doe. Rest in peace, Jane. Hello. My name is Strength. Hello. My name is Dignity. Hello. My name is Courage. Hello. My name is Barb Jenkins and you did not succeed in destroying me.

JANE DOE

---◆◆---

Who Is She?

I'm not the same girl anymore...
Pain changed me.

"I'm not the same girl anymore . . ."

Pain changed me.

I came as a weeping, broken mess and fell at my Father's feet. He gently lifted my head and held his arms out to me. I crawled up on his lap, as a child climbs on the lap of her daddy and put my head on his shoulder. He wrapped his arms around me, held me tightly, and let me cry. And I didn't just cry softly; I cried gut-wrenching bitterness of soul tears. Sobs wracked my body, and the river seemed to have no end. After a while, he soothed me with his words, "Hush now. I am here, and I love you. You are going to be okay. I promise."

No, I thought. I am *never* going to be okay again. I am broken. I am useless. I am unclean, degraded, ugly. I am damaged goods. How will anyone ever look at me the same again? Now that they know what happened to me, will they still love me? Will they want to be around me? How am I supposed to be now? I felt completely unworthy of the title of wife and mom. Even more than those titles, I felt stripped of my identity as a Christian woman. I wanted to disappear! I truly wished I was dead. Little did I know I had just joined the ranks of the "living dead."

Jane Doe. That's me now. People don't know my name. They don't know my face. All they know is what the newspaper decided to tell them about me. But who is she, really? Well, she's not just the nameless woman at the morgue. She's not just the faceless woman you hear about on the evening news whose body was found in some dark alleyway, abandoned house, or even some well-known park.

So who is she then? She is someone you know very well. She is someone who is living with the stigma and shame of being "Jane Doe." Maybe she has been assaulted as a child, or maybe she was a teen. It could be she was a young adult, or even a middle-aged woman. And, yes, maybe she is even the grandmother down the street. Even worse, maybe she is someone who has been in multiple stages of life when she was assaulted. She is more familiar than you imagine.

Jane Doe is one of three to four women in your life! She's the woman next door, she's your best friend, she's your coworker, she's your sister, she's your mother or grandmother. She could be the woman at the bank, a lawyer, doctor, dry cleaner, day care provider, your niece, your aunt, the store clerk, your vet, and, yes, even the lady you go to church with. Fill in the blank. That's her. Jane Doe exists because somebody stole her name and left her for dead.

To me, Jane Doe has always been the mystery woman in the "whodunit" movie or TV show. She was usually a victim of some hideous crime that someone had carried out on her. Usually a rape victim, she was left for dead or tortured to death. She maybe had a look of horror in her vacant eyes that plead with the viewer to find her tormentor and bring justice about for her sake.

Maybe she is a castoff from society. You know, the type of woman who learns really young that it can be an adrenaline rush to play it dangerous. You know her. She dresses recklessly, and her language is less than flattering. She is uneducated, having dropped out from high school or perhaps even earlier! Then she gets hooked on drugs or alcohol, or maybe she just goes from one meaningless relationship to the other, looking for something she never really finds. Nobody really knows her, and few care when they read that another prostitute has died at the hands of some unknown suspect.

Isn't that what you think too? I know what you mean. The truth is, there are a lot of "walking dead" in this life. Wounded souls. Some find the inner strength to pull themselves up by their proverbial bootstraps and go on as though Jane isn't a part of who they are. Then there are others who never get over having Jane be a part of who they are. Nobody, and I do mean nobody, ever asked to be Jane Doe. Jane is the cozy label put on the ones who have experienced an earth-shattering experience of sexual violence against them. For privacy and protection, and by the very nature of how she came to be, Jane overshadows the previous person. Whoever Jane was before gets lost in the shuffle. And therein lies the premise for this book.

I am Jane Doe. I am not your typical Jane Doe. I am married, and at the time of me becoming Jane, I was forty-eight years old and had just celebrated my silver anniversary with my husband with a wonderful celebration of us in Charleston, South Carolina. My life was good, and my marriage and family were healthy. My son was twenty, and my daughter nearly fifteen. Our life was charmed. We did our usual thing: hubby and I going to our respective jobs from Monday through Friday and our kids going to their respective schools—our son at the University of Montana and our daughter at one of the local high schools. We did the normal family activities, including attending church every Sunday with me and hubby singing on the praise team and our kids doing the things they do to fit in. Our home was filled with silliness and laughter and close relationships. That is not to say we didn't have our issues at times, but all in all, we were your "average" American family living out the average dream.

When you really sit down to study the facts about the Jane Does of this world, it is staggering. I already pointed out one in three or four women are victims of some form of sexual assault or rape. One-third! Every two minutes, someone in America is assaulted. That is approximately 720 assaults a day, 5,040 a week, 20,160 per month, and nearly 242,000 per year! And that is just our country! Think about that, and really let it soak in. That is a huge amount of our population. Sadly, though, only a little under 350 of 1,000 people even report that they are a victim of a violent crime. Unfortunately, I know firsthand why.

When you have a population of 325,146,000 in this country alone and you have an average of 242,000 people per year being assaulted, what does this give you? A recipe for a lot of hurting people, i.e., Jane Does, walking around trying to find themselves after they have been left for dead, either physically, mentally/emotionally, or spiritually. I am not trying to ignore that the male population is a part of this equation, but for my purposes, I will concentrate on women since they make up the largest portion of the sexually abused.

Women who are victims of incest, rape, or abuse are at elevated risk for PTSD. Post-traumatic stress disorder is not just for soldiers and those returning home from war. No, in fact, 93 percent of women have PTSD from sexual violence against them, 33 percent of women contemplate suicide, and 13 percent attempt suicide after rape. I myself, unfortunately at one time or another, fit into all three of these categories.

Being Jane Doe carries with it a special kind of loneliness reserved just for us. Nobody really understands how you feel unless they have been there themselves. But there is hope. The more we as Jane Doe can speak of our experiences, the more we can help each other and educate the public, and the less power Jane will have over us. Rather than hate Jane, we need to learn to love her and accept her as our Father in heaven loves and accepts us, warts and all.

Jane is a wounded creature. She has deep, agonizing hurt inside her. She is misunderstood, judged, lonely, confused, full of trauma, and suffers from deep depression often leading to thoughts of suicide and often blames herself for her circumstances. She self-medicates using alcohol or drugs, or maybe she eats to comfort the inner person, or maybe she shops uncontrollably, looking for a way to dull the ache inside. Her self-loathing takes on many forms, and each coping mechanism she has may not be the best for her, but she uses them anyway. Whatever form of coping Jane takes, it is the only way she knows how to manage until she can finally find healing.

Jane may be walking around with a smile on her face. She does that sometimes. She feels the need to hide, so she wears a mask to the public and even to her own family waiting for her at home. It is self-preservation. She must hold it all together since everybody needs her strong and present. If she lets down the guard, her raw pain causes others to hurt, and that in itself is another form of torture. So she hides in the shower and cries there where nobody will see it, or she silently cries herself to sleep.

The road to healing is long and hard. It really is up to each and every Jane Doe to decide how long she will live with the label and stigma of having that identity. Trauma and PTSD do not have a uniform look to them. If they did, we could have a fast cure all, and it would be a part of our past we don't need to think about. But that is just not reality. It takes a great deal of strength and courage for Jane to get up off the ground and dust herself off. It takes a great deal less courage and strength to let the horrible blackness swallow her whole.

Let's take a quick look at what *Webster* defines *trauma* as

> 1. (a) An injury (as a wound) to living tissue caused by an extrinsic agent; (b) a disordered psychic or behavioral state resulting from severe mental or emotional stress or physical injury; (c) an emotional upset <the personal *trauma* of an executive who is not living up to his own expectations—Karen W. Arenson>

> 2. An agent, force, or mechanism that causes trauma

And now let's look at what *Webster* has to say about PTSD:

> 1. A psychological reaction occurring after experiencing a highly stressing event (as wartime combat, physical violence, or a natural disaster) that is usually characterized by depression, anxiety, flashbacks, recurrent nightmares, and avoidance of reminders of the event—abbreviation *PTSD*—called also *post-traumatic stress syndrome*

It seems rather cold to put it in such black-and-white terms. Trauma is such an interesting and insensitive beast. This kind of trauma colors how you view the world and how you interact with others. It is a form of prison for the soul, leaving you searching for meaning and comfort, love and light. We carry the images, the feelings, the smells, the sounds, and all the emotional overload that go along with the trauma with us into our daily lives.

When we experience such things as PTSD and trauma, those around us and those we reach out to also experience a form of it as well. Secondary trauma is very real too. Our family members, the medical professionals we seek out, the counselors, the police, the attorneys, our closest friends, and our spiritual mentors all feel a form of this trauma. If we are not careful, this can really shift our viewpoint of the world and stymy the ability to see the world through any other lens but the trauma lens.

Jane walks through this life as a sort of half person. She feels shattered inside, lost and unable to function as a "normal" person should. Little things may freak her out, such as simply walking into a store or going out to eat. Sometimes, the fear is overwhelming, and she can feel like everyone is looking at her and talking about her and like she is being looked at as "less than" what she was before. Judgment is sure to be in the forethought of Jane's mind, regardless of how true or not true that reality is at the time.

Certain colors, objects, or places can bring about an instant panic to Jane. Depending on her circumstances when she was violated or traumatized in the first place, it can be anything that sets her back to that moment when she lost herself as someone else took what wasn't theirs to take. It is at these times that she feels absolutely desperate to find peace, serenity, and calm in the storm. It is also these times when Jane needs the most compassion and empathy she can get—both externally and internally.

I am here to tell you that it is possible to learn to live with Jane. It is possible to let Jane fade to the background, and the person she overshadowed can come alive again. This needs to be a deliberate process. There is no right or wrong timeline for any Jane Doe, but the path back does start when you take the first step, even tiptoeing if you must.

This long and difficult journey begins with Jane reaching out to any and all resources available to her to find her way back to life before trauma. It means reading to understand what is going on inside, it means journaling to get it out, it means talking to professionals to help you sort it out, and it means finding a relationship with God who loves you immeasurably and does not want to see you hurt. It means praying a lot. It means treating yourself with kindness, compassion, and patience. It means trusting your friends and family enough to let them in to see the brokenness and let them help you stand up and live a vibrant and purpose-filled life again. It means reprogramming your thoughts to positive affirmation and tuning out the negative affirmations.

This is the true story of my personal journey. I know it may not be easy for some to read, but it will be relatable. I am certain I am supposed to write about this experience because there appears to be no real communication about being Jane Doe and how to let go of her and be *you* again. So read on and be encouraged. Don't be afraid to let yourself explore some of the coping mechanisms that are healthier for you. Never feel like you are alone. You are never, ever alone. The Lord says, "Never will I leave you, and never will I forsake you." This is a journey of trust. I chose to trust instead of giving in to the black hole of suffering that threatened me and my family. You can too.

The first promise: "All things work together for good to those who love the Lord and are called according to his purpose" (Romans 8:28). Hard to swallow? Yes. But it is true. Trust. As a child, I fell at my Father's feet, broken and deeply wounded and hurt. The feeling of desperation that consumed me was, and is, inexplicable and unfathomable only to those who have never had to experience it. All I could manage to utter in prayer was, "Jesus." And that, my friend, is all it took to bring legions of angels to minister to my spirit and make me whole again. That one word uttered in childlike dependence and faith held more weight than all the other words I would articulate in the coming months. It did not happen overnight for me, and it won't happen overnight for you, but Jane Doe can be laid to rest.

Taking the first step toward an unknown future is the hardest. But if you don't lift your foot and make the first move toward hope, healing cannot follow.

—Anita Brooks

THE COMMISSIONED

---◆◆---

A Test of Obedience

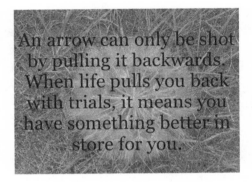

An arrow can only be shot by pulling it backward.
So when life is dragging you back with difficulties
It means that it's going to launch you into something great.

It was the year of 2013 when I distinctly felt the prompting of the Holy Spirit telling me what I needed to do. "Go and talk to *that* one." I argued with him saying he was scary, unapproachable, and intimidating; and he smelled terrible. But the Spirit was insistent, so I obeyed. I walked over to the table where this homeless man sat at the local day center that serviced the homeless population in Missoula, Montana.

"Hi. What is your name?" I sat for what seemed like an eternity while he sized me up. He literally pulled back in his chair, turned sideways, and studied me. Finally, he said his name in a barely audible voice. I asked him what he said again and apologized for not being able to understand him in his whispering voice. He once again studied me for a long time, then answered a little more audibly what his name was. "Johnathan."

I chatted nervously at him, rather than with Johnathan, for a few minutes before retreating to the kitchen to finish my duties. A male volunteer told me, "You're wasting your time with ole Johnathan. You will never get him to talk." I told him he was right, but just wait—God was about to do something! And he sure did.

Over the next weeks and months, we witnessed a metamorphosis of an extreme version of isolation and homelessness to a new creature. Each week, Johnathan would come in to the day center to eat his midday meal, and each time, I was there to greet him with a cheery greeting. I made it a point to sit at the table across from him for a few minutes each week to try and break down the barriers he had up and validate him as a person. I would tell him of my family and ask him open-ended questions to make him communicate with me. He was like a flower blooming, opening more and more each week. Even the patrons and other volunteers were astounded by this change happening before their eyes.

Johnathan smelled horrible. There was no other person who came in off the streets who smelled worse than Johnathan. All the other patrons of the day center would complain when he would come in, and make very rude comments. I don't know when the last time was he had had a real shower, let alone laundered his clothes. He lived in the same set of clothes day in and day out. His clothes were sheer rags and literally hung in strips on his body. Even so, after a few months, he would come into the day center and spend much time in the bathroom cleaning himself up. This was progress.

My heart was pierced to the core with wanting to help this poor man. He was so poverty stricken that even he didn't know the depth of his poverty. There is poverty of the body, yes, but there is also a poverty of the spirit that goes far beyond the poverty of the body.

I believe this is a far worse condition than anything I have ever seen anyone suffer with. Because of his condition, he was pretty much friendless. He didn't share his past with anyone, and he had no plans for a future. His existence was just that, an existence. It broke my heart to the point I was driven into action.

In the fall of 2013 and winter of 2014, I took to visiting a particular park where I knew there were a lot of homeless camps along the riverbank. I would take my lunch break at McCormick Park; and along with my best friend, Liz Newsom, I would walk along the bank of the river, praying for each obvious homeless camp and for all those whom we didn't know of. We did this faithfully for weeks. On the times my friend was unable to come with me, I went alone and continued to pray. It was on one of these occasions I ran across the camp of Johnathan. Once I knew where he "lived," I spent a considerable amount of time at his camp while he was gone, praying for him.

The winter of 2014 was a particularly nasty one, even for Montana. The temps were far below zero, and the snow was piled deeper than I had remembered seeing for years. I was consumed with worry for the homeless community here. I sprang into action, and with the help of a lot of women from my church, we made about seventy-five fleece blankets and gave them to those who were in desperate need for warmth. Johnathan was the recipient of one of these blankets, which he promptly gave away. I was frustrated at this but touched at the same time that he would give up his warmth for another's. He, of course, was given another blanket, which I told him sternly he would keep this time. He did.

I worried about Johnathan. Most of the homeless people had some form of shelter. They would live in tents or makeshift shelters or abandoned buildings, under bridges, even in garbage dumpsters; or they would go to the local homeless shelter and sleep in a corner if there was no bed available. The point is that nearly everyone had one goal, and that was to find shelter in some form to protect from the frigid subzero conditions and wind chill. In those temps, it was dangerous to live outside. It was dangerous to be outside at all for any length of time. Add the wetness of snow to the freezing temps, and you have a disaster waiting to happen. But Johnathan was too proud and too isolated from others to go to the homeless shelter to sleep, so he would lay out his wet and frozen sleeping bag and blankets and hunker in for the night.

Liz and I were touched by his lack of protection in the elements, so we purchased a new one-piece insulated Carhartt for him. We provided him with new insulated boots, wool socks, a new hat, gloves, a wool sweater, tarps, and even a tent. Of course, the tent was never used, and he gave that away. One of the most frustrating things we encountered helping Johnathan was his refusal to accept our gifts of comfort. We never knew if he would actually keep what was given to him or give it away because he "really didn't need it." In this case, he did keep the bulk of what we gave him and accepted it gratefully.

During this extreme weather, I found Johnathan in a state of hypothermia, digging through the snow behind the day center with his bare hands, which were bleeding. He was a shocking sight to behold. His beard, mustache, eyelashes, eyebrows, and hair were a solid chunk of ice. He had shed his coat and had no hat or gloves. His sweater was also full of ice chunks. I was terrified at what I saw and tried to get him to come inside. When I finally convinced him to come inside, the day center closed down due to a criminal who was on the loose who had just held up two businesses in the area.

I had to go to work, but I phoned his mom. She asked me to call 911, but I didn't, because he had disappeared after the center had shut down. So, after work that day, I set off on a hunt for Johnathan. I found him close to the day center digging furiously through the snow with his bare hands again. He was still a solid chunk of ice and was quite literally out of his mind. I got him into my car and phoned the executive director of the day center for advice. His advice was to take him to the hospital, his house, or a hotel.

I was able to communicate with Johnathan after a while and gave him his choice of where to go. He chose the hotel, so I purchased a room for him with strict instructions that he was to stay there. Liz ended up paying for him to stay there for over a month to keep him out of the most dangerous part of the winter. During this time, he was more like a normal man than I had ever seen him. He was calm, peaceful, and very grateful for the help. He knew his life had just been saved, and he couldn't thank us enough. At times, he would be overcome with feelings of gratitude and an inadequacy to repay the kindness shown to him. I used these opportunities to speak to him about Jesus and our own inadequacy to repay him for his saving grace to us.

Meanwhile, I was busy encouraging Johnathan to start the process to get off the streets. For a long time leading up to this nasty winter, I would ask Johnathan if he was ready to get off the streets and start to live again. At first, he would tell me no. Then he would tell me he was thinking about it. At last, he said that, yes, he was ready. So I jumped on board and started to help him through the lengthy process of getting into the programs that would help him. At this point, we were getting really close to being able to find him an apartment. He was now receiving food stamps, and his social security was about to begin. Things were really looking up for Johnathan.

It was St. Patrick's Day of 2014 when I got a phone call from Johnathan's brother. I had been in contact with Johnathan's family and telling them of the good that was happening in his life. They were beyond grateful for someone taking an interest in him and thankful for the communication on his progress. Johnathan's brother informed me that day that their mother had died suddenly of a heart attack. She was young, and her death was premature. Johnathan's brother didn't know where to find him and asked my help. Up until this point, I had not met any of his family; I had only communicated via phone with their mother.

I went to the hospital where several family members had gathered and where they were preparing for the sad task of removing life support for their mother, who was an organ donor. Johnathan's brother was en route from North Dakota, where he was working in the oil industry. I asked the family if they would like me to go get Johnathan, but they said no; they wanted to wait for his brother to return so I could take him down to the river and let him give the unfortunate news.

The next morning, I met Johnathan's brother at the park where I knew we would find Johnathan. He was a kind man and very appreciative toward me. I led him to the spot along the river where Johnathan was camped and found him asleep. I gently tapped him on the shoulder and spoke to him. I startled him awake, and when he saw his brother, he was instantly angry asking me why I brought "that guy" down there. I told him sternly it was his brother and he needed to sit up as he had something important to tell him. His brother then told him of his mother's death. I watched him closely to see how he would respond to this news. He surprisingly had very little reaction. He just nodded a lot and then told his brother he loved him, and they embraced.

The next week was a bit of a flurry between funeral preparation and worry over the mental stability of Johnathan. By now, I had spent enough time with Johnathan to know that he was suffering with mental illness. But the thing about him was he did not equate himself as a mentally ill man, so treatment was next to impossible with his denial. He was completely capable of acting like a normal person, but then sometimes he would go off on a tangent, leaving the listener in a state of shock. It was quite a trip to be around Johnathan in these moments.

The day of Johnathan's mother's funeral was here. I purchased some clothing and a pair of shoes for Johnathan that would be more appropriate for him to wear. Our church put him in a hotel for the night so he could have a good rest and a shower before the service. He was clean and had his normally wild hair and beard brushed and looking good. He managed to communicate pretty well with all the relatives who had come from all over the states. Most had not seen him for over thirteen years, the length of time he had started living on the streets. They were all so gracious toward me and in a state of awe at the transformation that had taken place. I kept encouraging his family to keep praying and not give up, as God was listening and answering their prayers.

I sat with Johnathan and his family and hovered over him like a mother hen that day. At one point, he put himself in a closet. I wasn't sure if he was just overwhelmed by the people or if he needed a private place to cry. For sure, when I went after him, I found him in tears. It was the first sign of any emotion I had seen since the news of his mother's death. Really, I think it was the first time I had really seen *any* kind of deep emotion come from him. He said he was sad in his tummy. This is something I would learn as time went on, that Johnathan would talk of his feelings "through his tummy." I convinced him he needed to come out of the closet, or his family would start to worry. He came out and did well from there on out and ended the day by going to his brother's place and hanging out for a while with family. This too was a small miracle as he continually had denied himself spending time with family for any reason and also would not accept any help they tried to give him.

Johnathan was only a few weeks out from getting an apartment when spring came. I convinced him to purchase a cell phone because he was getting harder and harder to contact. At this point, he had formed a relationship with an older woman and was spending most of his nights at her place. I had no idea who she was or where she lived, so I had to leave messages for him at the day center and hope he would go there to eat so he could get his messages. Once he had a phone, things were much easier.

One morning, I went down to Johnathan's camp, which had to be moved up along the bank of the river due to backwaters and spring runoff. I wanted to notify him of an appointment to view an apartment. When I was done delivering my message to him, he pinned me up against the bushes and groped me and ground into me with his pelvis. I was really upset at his behavior and left the park in a state of shock. I rationalized his behavior thinking he had acted out as a result of the turmoil he was in over the loss of his mother. The next time I spoke to him, I warned him he was not to do that again. I was really mad at him, and he was extremely apologetic to me. I mentioned to his caseworker that he had crossed the line with me, and she counseled me to try and wean away from him, which I started to do.

Things were going along fine. Johnathan was able to rent an apartment even though he had no previous rental history. One property management company was willing to give him a break and help him rebuild his life. He seemed very happy to have an apartment and would often tell me how grateful he was and say he didn't know how to repay me. I always told him to keep moving forward and never go back. I also reminded him that he needed to thank God because it was God who was in control and it was God who was helping him.

Liz and I would visit Johnathan often. We would make it a point to take him to lunch or to do his laundry or to get food from the store since he had no transportation. We even took him to get his first Christmas tree and helped him decorate it as we listened to Christmas music and sang along. He seemed very pleased. I asked him what he would like for Christmas, and he was adamant he wanted a cross to put up on his wall.

I purchased a really nice cross for Johnathan for Christmas. I was really pleased he wanted to have something to remind him of Jesus and his love for him. I was excited to see him open it and wondered where he would place it in his apartment. I never saw him open the gift. After Christmas and New Year's were over, I went to his place to help him undecorate the tree and store his ornaments. I noticed that the cross was nowhere to be seen, so I asked him about it. He said he broke it into little pieces and "gave it to the ants out back." I was really hurt by this but tried to not show it. I felt he was rejecting God but trying to hurt me in the process, and I didn't understand why.

That day when I got ready to leave, he walked me to the door, but then he locked it and pushed me up against the door with his pelvis and assaulted me as before. I was able to talk him down and left his apartment before he could do anything more. This attack affected me deeply; and I was really shaken, scared, and very hurt by his actions. It was at this time I sought out help from the local YWCA. I also contacted his new case manager and reported the incident to him. But because I was unwilling to go to the police with this attack, I was, henceforth, cut off from communication with the WMMHC (Western Montana Mental Health Center) regarding Johnathan and his circumstances. This was a blow to me as well, since up until this incident, I was praised highly for my advocacy and the friendship I had so freely offered Johnathan. I felt very abandoned by this act of unprofessionalism and was insulted at this treatment.

I was severely torn at this point. I still felt I was to help Johnathan, but I no longer trusted him. I tried to help him by encouraging him from afar. I would send him encouraging notes or cards, and I would call him and check up on him to make sure he was making his appointments and paying his bills. He would say he wanted to see me, but I would make excuses to not be around him unless we were in a very public place. For a time, I would meet him once a week for lunch until he blasted me with an entourage of profanity and wild statements and accusations. I left him sitting in the restaurant and told him I would not do that anymore because of his actions.

It was clear Johnathan was on the decline. He had stopped bathing and had stopped laundering his clothing. He would shut his power off to the kitchen appliances, saying the refrigerator was too loud and the stove's "face" kept staring at him. He and his apartment smelled horrid. He would not throw away the guts of his vegetables such as green peppers and would instead leave them inside the cupboard, growing nasty mold on them; or he would line them up along the wall outside the garbage can. He would blow off his appointments and talk of having dead people living under his apartment. He would spend hours in his apartment with the shades pulled and dark blankets over the windows and simply sit in the dark. He would not watch TV and barely listened to a radio he was given. It was just not healthy, and I worried for him. He was sliding backward in a hurry, and I was powerless to do anything to reach him.

Johnathan would imagine that people were breaking into his apartment, dousing it with gasoline, tipping the furniture over, cutting him under his fingernails with razor blades, and various other things that made no sense. At one point, his neighbor contacted me because he found him outside in the middle of the night naked while rolling up the hoses for the apartment. He was worried that maybe he was a sexual predator and the neighborhood might not be safe. When I questioned Johnathan about this event, he didn't really respond.

As always, Johnathan was repentant toward me after he had had any kind of negative outbursts or behavior that was unacceptable. Johnathan simply was not willing to acknowledge that I was not interested in him as anything other than a friend or even as a sort of mother/son-type relationship. When he would bring the subject up, I would remind him how much I loved my family and the Lord, and how I wished he would find a woman he could have a close romantic-type relationship with. I would encourage him telling him most women need security and, until he was able to hold a job down, he most likely would not find a woman willing to live like he was living. He would always agree with me and would talk about what he might do as a vocation.

All throughout my time helping Johnathan, I spent considerable time in prayer, asking God to protect, guide, and help me to know how to help him. I prayed for his soul and that God would find a way to prick his heart so he would finally be able to be healed of the demons that he was fighting. It seemed that the more I prayed for Johnathan and the more he would start to change, and then the more the devil would start to attack, and it was always directed at me.

By August of 2015, I had cut communication entirely with Johnathan. He simply would not respect my boundaries, and I felt I had no other choice but to cut communication. I ignored his many phone calls and texts for an entire month. He then reached out to me while I was at work and bombarded me with foul language and wild accusations. I was insulted and hung up on him to which he phoned back. I threatened him at this point that I would call the police if he called my work again.

He didn't call my work number again, but he did call my cell phone incessantly seven times in a row, which I never answered. He ended up leaving me five ranting voice mails, each about two to three minutes long. It was at this point I decided I had no other choice but to place a restraining order on him, so I did. It went into effect for a year at the end of August. I felt absolutely horrible about this, but I also felt I had no other choice. I needed to find protection from him as he was certainly not a safe person for me to be around any longer.

The day Johnathan was served the order of protection, he vacated his apartment and went incognito. It was the day the judge signed the order that he showed up, and I was shocked to see he had cut all his hair off and shaved his face completely. I barely even recognized him. I stood around the corner, not wanting to be near him when he came and stood across from me. He said, "Barbie, I am really sorry. I shouldn't have left you those voice mails. I don't want to cause you or your family any problems." I simply told him that it was too late for sorry now, and he needed to accept that. I then went to the office and asked them to keep him away from me. He didn't contest the judge's decision, and I thought that was the end of that.

I was wrong.

There is a moment in each person's life where they come to a point of decision. This is called a kairos moment. It is a defining moment in time. You have before you two roads to travel. Either one will lead you down a path unknown, a future in unchartered territory. The word is Greek meaning "opportunity," "season," or "fitting time." Johnathan was about to come to his kairos moment, and my life would be forever changed.

Johnathan was raised by a God-fearing woman. He knew who God was and was in fact very capable of quoting biblical truths and scriptures. He sat through the Bible studies I had led at the day center and also attended many other studies there with other people leading them. He was not ignorant when it came to the word of God. He had a good sense in the difference between right and wrong. I had spent many hours talking with Johnathan, so I knew this to be true. When he would wrestle with his conscience, he knew that was actually God telling him what he needed to do to be "right" with him. I believe this is what motivated him to always apologize to me for his words and actions that were hurtful and destructive to me.

But here's the thing. Regardless of how each of us are raised, what our faith beliefs are and what our standard of moral and clean living is, the bottom line is we are all given that wonderful thing called free will. God will not lead anyone into temptation, and he will not leave us or forsake us, ever. The problem exists when in our own hearts, we are enticed by evil thoughts, and they spring into evil actions.

Johnathan had been blessed. He was given a good friend who really cared about his well-being and his soul. He had an advocate willing to go to bat for him. He found another human being who looked inside him and saw a person, not a homeless vagrant in rags but a real-life hurting person. For the first time in a long time, someone believed in him and saw his potential. And he just couldn't handle it. He was faced with a crossroads. Which way he chose would determine the future, and he was well aware of this fact.

When we do our acts of service for mankind in the name of God, we are not merely showing our love to man who is made in God's image but to God himself. Our acts of kindness, compassion, and love are because he placed that within us all to share with others and to lead others back to him. Love like that is a beautiful thing, and no flaming darts of Satan can destroy that kind of beauty. He may maim us or kill our bodies, but he can't destroy our relationship to the Father unless we give him permission to.

Promise number two: "Never will I leave you. Never will I forsake you" (Hebrews 13:5). Some say when destruction comes into their life that God is "doing this to" them. This stems from a wrong ideal of who the real character of God is. He does not take joy or delight in any of his children's suffering. And when he promises something, He never goes back on his word. Once again, it is a trust journey. Our job is to live our lives in service to him. He never promised the road would be easy. In fact, he guarantees it won't be easy. But, nevertheless, he is always there, each step of the way.

THE LOSS

---◆◆---

Ultimate Identity Theft

Hardships often prepare ordinary people for an extraordinary destiny.

— Unknown

The morning was an unimaginably beautiful, crisp, and clear fall day. The sky was incredible with the trademark "Big Sky Montana" blue, stretching as far as the eye could see. The events of the previous week plagued my mind, and the more I thought of it, the more I was convinced of what I needed to do. I needed to confront my threat face-to-face.

Nobody had heard from Johnathan from the day since we saw him at the courthouse and the judge signed that order of protection. His family didn't have any communication with him, and, thankfully, he didn't try to call me anymore. All communication was, at long last, ceased. He didn't go into the day center as far as I knew (neither did I), and he was not seen around town. I had convinced myself that he simply moved apartments and was merely holed up.

It was the first week of October. I was down in the park as was my habit. I would spend my lunch breaks walking the walking path between the pool and the university. It was a quick five kilometers and easily doable in the one hour I had for my lunch break. I still said silent prayers for the inhabitants of this park. Sometimes I would sit by the pond and meditate, and sometimes I would walk through the park to a certain part I used to love to go to for some quiet time of reflection. I craved being outside and loved the exercise.

I marvel at creation, especially in the autumn months. I love the color of the trees, the crispness of the air, the smell of the leaves after they wake with the dew on them each day. I love the rustle of the leaves under my feet as I walk through them. In all honesty, I could still spend hours building a leaf tunnel system and burrowing through them just as I did when I was kid. It is my favorite season! My heart is at one with God when I can spend time outside.

On one occasion, I was walking along the riverbank. My sweet counselor at the YWCA had suggested I take sticks and toss them into the river as a means to healing. I would pick one up and toss it into the river, saying, "This is for the time when you did ———— ————." I would watch them float away and think of how my pain was symbolically floating away too. It was therapeutic and a way for me to essentially "let go" of the pain Johnathan had caused me. This particular day I literally ran into Johnathan.

As I pondered what to do, I was struck by the calm demeanor of Johnathan. He seemed like he was at peace more than the previous months when I was still in touch with him. I wondered if he was indeed homeless again and took note of his appearance. I started to leave and Johnathan spoke to me. In regard to the order of protection, he should have turned around and walked away. But instead he wanted to talk to me. He once again apologized to me for his behavior. I asked him if he was homeless again, and he confirmed he was. I asked him if he was trying to get back into housing, and he said he was not sure how to go about it. I suggested maybe Liz would be willing to help him.

My heart was sad. All that effort and time seemed to be a giant colossal failure. I wondered what would become of Johnathan now. He had burned all his bridges, and there didn't seem to be any avenue open to him. Just the same, I reminded myself that he made a choice to live that way.

I left the park that day and thought about the chance meeting. I chalked it up to just that—a fluke meeting. The next day, however, I was on my usual jaunt between the pool and the university with my earbuds in my ears, listening to my Christian music. I became aware of heavy-sounding footsteps behind me. I turned around and was shocked to see that Johnathan was running after me. I was startled by this and a little unnerved by it.

He asked me if I would sit down and talk to him. My immediate reaction was to say no. I reminded him there was a restraining order against him. "Was that *your* idea?" he asked me. "Yes. You left me no choice."

He was persistent in asking me to sit down and let him talk to me. I finally agreed and sat across from him at a picnic table. He began by telling me once again how sorry he was that he had hurt me. He said he regretted the phone calls and his behavior toward me. He talked about me and my family and how he didn't want to hurt me. He kept saying I was such a "good, good lady." I told him I appreciated that, and I offered my forgiveness and left the park.

I came home and told my husband about the events of the last two days. He was very unhappy with me for not reporting the breach of the order of protection. I thought he was overreacting as I ratio-nalized once again that he didn't hurt me, all he did was talk. How bad could it really be, right? It just so happened that my husband needed to leave for business. He would be in Las Vegas for several days at a trade show, and I had the day off that Monday in honor of Columbus Day. In the time he was gone, I sat and really pondered over the two meetings I had had with Johnathan.

As I did often, I took a jog the night before that fateful day. Running is a wonderful way for me to escape and to clear my head. I love the sense of accomplishment when I can run a longer dis-tance and not get overwhelmed by the effort. I needed that release of endorphins. I would plug in my music and commune with my God as I ran. I got about a mile or so away from our home on my way back when my left foot suddenly was in so much pain I could barely put weight on it. I called my son and asked him to come pick me up, which he did.

The pain was incredible. I didn't roll my ankle, and I had on good running shoes. I didn't remember stepping on some uneven ground and couldn't figure out what was wrong with my foot. It felt like the whole bottom of my foot was torn. I sustained previous injuries to my feet and ankles, so I drug out the dreaded crutches and tried to maneuver with them. It did help, but crutches are so clumsy!

While running, praying, and pondering, I concluded that Johnathan was most likely looking for me those two days. I decided in that moment that I needed to go find Johnathan and, this time, I would initiate a conversation. I felt he needed to hear from me and me alone. I wanted to look him in the eyes and confirm to him that this was my decision to not have anything to do with him and it was a firm and final decision. I had helped him all I could, and my hands were completely tied. I could do no more. Furthermore, now that I realized that he most likely was living down in that park again, I would no longer be there, so he need not look for me.

And so, it was on that beautiful fall morning when my life would never be the same again, and for that matter, neither would Johnathan's. My mind was busy thinking about if I would find him where I thought he might be and what I was going to say to him.

I wondered if it would be a short and concise conversation or if he would go on another tangent toward me. But never once did it occur to me that things would go the way they did. That kairos moment was only moments away.

I arrived down at the park and maneuvered about with my crutches. It was very painful to walk on my left foot, even with the crutches. Any pressure and my body screamed at me. I made my way down the walking path to the place where I believed Johnathan might be, and sure enough, I found him there. I hollered out to him and made my way down to the riverbank beach. It was an awkward trip down the slope of the bank to get there with my crutches and the unevenness of the ground. He was surprised to see me and especially with the crutches.

I led off the conversation. "I am not here for long. I just felt I needed to talk to you face-to-face." He had a blanket on the ground and offered me a place to sit. I did sit down, relieved to not have to deal with my foot. I tucked my legs to my chest and held my arms around my knees, crutches beside me on the ground. Before I spoke again, Johnathan excused himself to the other side of the beach to use the bathroom. He didn't bother to try and hide from anyone. I sat in uneasiness as I waited for him, rehearsing what I was to say and averting my eyes from his direction.

When Johnathan came back, he asked me about the crutches. I told him I was jogging the night before and how I had somehow injured my foot. He reached over and squeezed my foot and watched me for a reaction. I grimaced and flinched and told him to stop as he was hurting me. He did.

I looked at him right in the eyes and started my speech. "I felt I needed to come and talk to you face-to-face. I have thought a lot about how you were here the last two times I came here. I think you were looking for me. I have done everything I can for you. I helped you in many ways, including getting food stamps, social security, Medicaid, an apartment, and all the furnishings, and I tried to help you succeed. I encouraged you, and I gave you my friendship. But you didn't respect my boundaries, and you overstepped where you shouldn't have. I want you to know that now that I know for sure you are living back down here I will never come back to this park again. So you need not look for me anymore, because I simply will not be here. You need to live the life you have chosen for yourself, and you need to let me live mine and respect the order of protection by not contacting me from here on out."

"You have beautiful eyes. You are such a good, good lady. You have beautiful hair. Your ears are beautiful. You are a good, good lady. Your smile is beautiful. Your body is beautiful."

"Johnathan, my body is not for you to admire or talk about that way. It is for my husband."

"Your legs are perfect. You are just so beautiful. You're such a devout and good, good lady." He was not listening and kept talking about all my body parts. I tried again. "Johnathan, you know that my body is not for you to look at or talk about like that. My body belongs to my husband and only my husband."

He looked at me for a few seconds, and I said I needed to go. I was feeling really uneasy. He got up on one knee next to me and reached over and removed my glasses from my face. Then he put his hand over my eyes and pulled my head into his armpit.

He was forcefully petting my head. I could feel my hair pulling out, and I could not breathe. The stench from Johnathan's body was overwhelming. I pulled my head up finally and tried to breathe cleaner air. "What are you doing Johnathan? Stop! You are hurting me!"

Johnathan then straddled my legs, sitting on my thighs. He was trying repeatedly to pull my shirts off me. He pulled his dirty T-shirt off and, without a word, continued to try and take my shirts off. I was moving my legs trying to get him off me, scared out of my wits as I could clearly see his intention at this point.

Somehow, I managed to get him off me, and I stood up and grabbed my crutches. My face was feeling flushed, and I was more scared of Johnathan than I had ever been before at that point. I looked at him and said, "I need to leave right now." His response to me was to step in front of me and back me into a large log. He said, "Well, I have you pinned against this log, and you're crippled, so ... " He used his body to back me into the log and started to grope me and grind into me with his pelvis. He was moaning and groaning and trying to kiss me. I kept turning my face away from him. He then looked at the walking path to my right and then back at me. He pulled my pants open and began to pull them down.

I was desperately trying to pull them back up, but he prevailed. I was begging him over and over, "Please, Johnathan, don't do this! Please don't do this," and "Please, Johnathan, *think* about what you are doing! Please *think*!" But he was not listening to me. He looked at me with his eyes half open and proceeded to rape me right there in public and broad daylight with me standing on my feet backed against a log. During the rape, I looked up and saw three people walking by on the walking path. I tried so hard to call out to them, but the only thing that would come out from my mouth was a whispered and quavering, "Please stop, Johnathan. Please just stop."

He was intently watching me while he was violating me. He thrust himself on me with heavy methodical force. I remember looking around trying desperately to disappear. This was not happening to me; it just couldn't be happening to me. This was not what I had envisioned when I came here. Oh, God, oh, God, please help me! My heart was pounding in fear, and my head was filled with fuzz and confusion and shock. My legs were lead filled, and I was paralyzed.

When he finished, he stepped back and put his hands down at his sides and just looked at me with no expression on his face. No shock. No remorse. No guilt. No consideration of me for what he had just carried out on me. I was sickened. My senses took it all in, and I was in vivid shock. I was also filled with an enormous amount of sheer hate at that moment. I hated him with every fiber of my being for what he did to me.

"You don't give a damn about me or anything!" "Yes, I do!" "No, you *don't*. You own this. I have to live with it, but *you* own this!" I pulled my pants back up, cognizant of the evidence of the release he left on me. I was shaking and barely able to move, but I made my way out of there. I was scared that he would follow me. I never looked back, but I could feel him watching me struggling up the riverbank back to the walking path.

I was tripping over my crutches, trying so hard to get out of that park as fast as I could. I truly didn't know if I was going to make it or not. I didn't trust Johnathan to not follow me or hurt me more. I passed a man going the other direction. I was crying and gasping for air and frustrated by my inadequacy in walking with the crutches. He had a quizzical look on his face, but he didn't ask if I was okay or offer me any help.

Finally, I reached my van where it was parked. I got into the van and locked the doors and cried. My mind was a blur, and I didn't know what to do. I had so many thoughts cascading through my brain, and I couldn't sort one from the other. I could not smell anything but the stench of Johnathan's armpit in my nose, and I felt the gross expulsion he had had on me, and I couldn't stand it. I needed to get clean, and it couldn't be soon enough.

The third promise: "The righteous cry out, and the Lord hears them; he delivers them from all their troubles. The Lord is close to the brokenhearted and saves those who are crushed in spirit. The righteous person may have many troubles, but the Lord delivers him from them all" (Psalm 34:17–19). One of the best advantages of being a Christian is knowing that no matter what happens, when we call on his name, he not only hears us, but he answers us. The avenue of prayer is a huge blessing that few really appreciate or understand. What kind of a God would he be if he could turn his ear away or not look in the direction of his child when we cry out to him in our brokenness?

THE WANDERER

Where Am I?

Numb. Head to foot numb. Shattered into a million pieces inside. Everything I was and believed about myself and the world was demolished in the few minutes it took Johnathan to rape me. My mind raced with all sorts of thoughts. "I should go to the police no yes No I don't know I should go wash myself off the stench is unbearable I should call my husband no I can't hurt him like this maybe I should kill myself no that is not the answer I should kill him I could do that I could go home grab the gun and go find him and shoot him straight in the head nobody would blame me no my kids need me oh how I *hate* him why did he do this to me why did I go down there it's my own fault *No it is not* I deserved this no I didn't I am so *stupid* I begged him to not do this I begged him over and over I can't stand how I feel he is responsible for this not me I should go to the police no I should just stay away don't say anything at all live with this and move on *No* If I do that he will do it again *Oh God why* why didn't he just kill me why did you allow him to do this to me *where are you* I hate him I hate me what am I going to do how can I live with this and not let this ruin me I feel so *dirty* I should call the police I should call someone *anyone* and tell them what happened no I can't I am so ashamed why did those people walk by and not help me I need to shower I feel *so* disgusting this smell makes me want to vomit *I want to die!*"

And so it went. My mind a racing mess and my senses on over-load with shock. I blindly drove out of the park not knowing if I would drive to the police station or home or off a road for that matter. I was feeling so much I couldn't feel anything. Tears poured from my eyes as I sobbed driving down the road. In all the time I had spent with Johnathan, I never dreamed his actions would be so completely dehumanizing to me. True, I had been in some tough situations with him, but I was always able to use my words to get him to back off. Why did I fail this time? Was it the finality in my voice that triggered him? I had spent so much time and energy building him up and val-idating his existence that my own was laid to waste. I was wounded deeply from this evil action carried out on me. I didn't know if I had it in me to pick myself up and move on. I wanted to die. Indeed, I wished I was dead.

I ended up driving myself all the way home. The desire to shower overpowered anything else in me. I simply could not stand another second of the stench of Johnathan on my body and the dev-astating feeling of his semen on me. I wanted it off me. I came home and sat down on the couch, crying uncontrollably, and my mind replayed the whole evil scene again and again. I desperately searched to see what I could have done differently to have avoided this, and I couldn't come up with anything other than not going down there in the first place.

After a few minutes, I went to the bathroom and took a hot shower. I was astounded to find that I could not remove his stench from my body and my nose. No amount of soap, no amount of rewashing—I couldn't purge my body of his foul and putrid scent. I was also shocked to find out no matter how much I tried, I also could not remove the feel of his secretion from my body. No matter what I did, I felt it there. My body was clean, but yet my body was desolated, and I hated it. I threw my capri jeans and my panties and the shirts I was wearing into the washing machine. Just touching them after I had showered made me want to shower again. It seemed there was no way for me to purify myself.

I spent the afternoon on the couch in a state of disbelief. My kids came home from school, and although they could tell I was obviously upset and asked what was wrong, they didn't press me for details thinking that I had maybe had an argument with their dad or something. Both were busy doing homework and getting ready to go to their activity for the evening. Not wanting to be too obvious about what I was going through, I told them I was sleepy and was going to go take a nap and excused myself to my bedroom. Both came to say good-bye to me, and I hugged them and then was alone again.

That day will forever be etched in my brain. There has never been a time in my life where I felt so completely demolished as a person. I have lived with a lot of trauma in my life. As a child, I lived in a home where abuse was not only present but prevalent. It seems the faces would change, and the form would change, but the end result was always the same. I was not a person, just some object to which someone would hurt. I felt discarded and worthless. I had no self-esteem to speak of and struggled to fit in. Despite the situations growing up, I managed to turn out okay. I believe in the end it was my faith that helped me rise above the personal tornadoes that routinely rocked my life. But this new injury was about to undo me. People who have been exposed to multiple episodes of trauma have a breaking point. This was mine. I was truly at ground zero, and I wished I had gone down in the collapse with the rubble of my soul, never to breathe again. I was not sure I even had the energy to try and rise up again. I was broken.

That night, I had a fitful and sleepless night. I would barely start to fall asleep, and I would immediately be transported to the beach and relive the whole terrible ordeal. I felt it over and repeatedly like a bad horror movie stuck on instant replay. I would fall asleep and have nightmares of being ravaged repeatedly while people jeered at me. I found myself running and in perpetual motion in my dreams but not going anywhere. People were staring at me as I stood there with my pants down below my hips while I tried unsuccessfully to pull them up, and Johnathan was just looking at me with dead half-open eyes and no expression on his face. I would cry out in my nightmares and wake up with sobbing and lamenting. I had fallen into a deep hole of emptiness and despair that would be with me for months. Each time I closed my eyes, I would see the look that Johnathan had in his eyes before and during the attack. I could smell him everywhere, and the stench overpowered me. I could feel his breath on my face and feel his hands on my body and was acutely aware of how much he was watching me for a reaction. All I could do was cry. And I tried to call out to God, but no words could come from my mouth. Even so, I knew in my heart that he knew and he was there with me, holding me, comforting me.

The morning finally arrived, and I had to pull myself together and go to work. I dreaded being around people. I didn't want to talk to anyone, and I didn't want to look at anyone because I knew if I did they would know instantly what had happened. I also knew if I did look someone in the eyes, I would most likely break down in tears. Those who know me well can always tell when something is wrong, because I was always a happy and bubbly outgoing type of person.

I looked in the mirror and barely recognized what I was seeing reflected. My face was puffy and red, and my eyes were nearly swollen shut from lack of sleep and an abundance of crying. I knew that no amount of makeup would fix this, and I knew that people would know something had gone terribly wrong with me. I couldn't believe what I had just experienced and was still unsure of how I should proceed. I vacillated back and forth about going to the police. I knew I didn't have the ability to pretend everything was okay. Not this time.

I dragged myself to the office and attempted to go about my day as normally as I could. My coworker noticed I was not okay and asked me if everything was all right. I told him I had a rough night, and he dismissed it. I sat in my office and broke down multiple times in tears. I went into the bathroom to try and mop up my eyes and clean my quickly disappearing mascara off my face. I was an emotional roller coaster and found it nearly impossible to be present and professional.

There is a man here in Missoula people call the "Candy Man." He had a habit of coming into our office every day and going to everyone and handing them a piece of candy. He was always cheerful, but I always found him to be a bit creepy. He didn't really seem to have a filter and would sometimes say some pretty inappropriate things to me and others. I didn't appreciate it but put up with it since he had a traumatic brain injury.

That day, I had zero tolerance for the Candy Man, and the last thing I needed was to hear anything remotely off-color directed at me. He came in as usual and stood at my door. I didn't look up at him but told him flatly, "Leave my office." He responded in some way, and I told him more forcefully, "Get out! Leave my office now!" He then put a couple pieces of candy on my desk and made some stupid comment, calling me "babe," to which I responded by picking the candy up and throwing it at him.

This, of course, got the attention of one of my bosses, who was instantly annoyed at me, but I didn't care. I grabbed my things and left the office. I didn't stop to explain to anyone what I was going through. I simply said, "I can't handle this right now. I need to leave!" I just knew I had to get out of there as the walls were closing in on me. I left the office and got into my car and drove around, trying to gather my thoughts. I couldn't quit crying. I was in severe shock, and my spirit hurt so deeply inside I could barely breathe. I drove downtown around the police station and debated if I should go in. I drove by the Crime Victims Advocate Office (CVA) multiple times and tried to decide what to do. I eventually went back to the office, but nobody asked me what my issue was or where I had been. They could tell I was in a really bad place and didn't know how to go about talking to me. I could hear them talking down the hall about how I flipped out and threw the candy at the Candy Man, but not understanding why I would do that.

Meanwhile, my friends from my church were texting me, asking me if I was going to come to lunch with them as we did each Tuesday. I largely ignored the text messages, and they just kept on coming. I knew I needed to have a good excuse to not go, and I couldn't come up with a good one, so I finally decided to go. I met them at Wendy's, but I was completely detached and spacey and unresponsive to the conversation around me. I could tell that they knew something was wrong, but I ignored the questions and stared out the window in a daze. I couldn't seem to form the words to tell them I had been raped. I was scared I would be judged and scared that I would lose the respect that they had for me.

I went back to my office again and sent a text to one of my friends who had gone to lunch that day. I asked her to come to my office as I really needed someone to talk to. She said it would be about an hour or so. I sat there for about fifteen minutes feeling completely numb. I had arrived at a decision, and I knew if I didn't do it now, I would not do it. I took a deep breath and told my boss I needed to go somewhere and didn't know if I would be back or not that day. He was clearly confused, concerned, and annoyed all at the same time but agreed to let me leave. I told him I would text him later.

I drove to the CVA and walked into the office. There was no turning back now. I was there to report the rape to the authorities. This was my first step in a long series of steps that would unfold before me. I was terrified. What if they didn't believe me? What if they thought I wanted this to happen? What would happen from here? Am I going to lose my marriage and my kids? My heart was beating in my ears. "Can I help you?" The lady behind the locked door and window was looking at me. I swallowed, took a deep breath, and said in a hushed tone, "I . . . I need to talk to someone. I need to report a sexual assault." My voice quavered, and my eyes welled up in tears. The lady took a look at me and came around to the door and opened it up. She led me to a room and asked me to have a seat, saying she would have someone come in shortly to visit with me. She was very kind and compassionate toward me. I still had doubts that I was doing the right thing, but it was too late to turn back now.

Before I knew it, a lady was joining me in the small comfortable room. I was offered a glass of water, which I accepted. She asked me questions, and I answered them, telling her the whole story from start to finish. She asked me then if I wanted to report this to the police, and I told her I did. Soon a lady officer came in and took my report. I was told the interview was being recorded. The room I was seated in was equipped with a camera that was used when anyone would come and want to make a police report of sexual attacks. After I told her my story, I was informed that I should go to First Step and have a rape kit done. Even though I had showered twice, it would be in my best interest to do so. She gave me some information on rape support in Missoula and told me the detective would be in touch within twenty-four hours to talk to me.

Meanwhile, my phone was going crazy. I had multiple calls and texts from my husband, who was in Las Vegas. He had tried to call me several times, and I turned my ringer off during the interviewing process at the CVA and with the police officer. He called my office, and my boss told him of my bizarre behavior and that he had no idea where I was. My boss began calling my phone too, trying to figure out what was going on with me. Also, my friend Ann Marie was calling me and had stopped by my office and visited with my boss. Both were very concerned about my well-being as Ann Marie had told him of my aloofness at our lady's lunchtime, and he had told her of my outburst that morning.

After I was done giving my original statement to the officer, I phoned my boss first, and I told him I had been attacked by Johnathan and that I was with the police. I didn't want to go into details with him, but he was very supportive and kind. It explained the day to him without words. Then I phoned Ann Marie and asked her to meet me at my office and go with me to see the First Step people. She knew what that meant without asking. I was really in need of support, and she came to meet me and take me there. I told her briefly on the phone I had been attacked by Johnathan. Then I got a call from my husband. I answered it.

"Barb, are you okay? I have been calling you all day long. Where have you been? What is going on?" I just started to cry. "Barb? Barb! You are scaring me. What is going on?" I dreaded telling him what had happened. I especially dreaded doing it over the phone, but I simply had no choice. I sobbed into the phone and in broken bits told him I had been attacked by Johnathan. He was incredibly upset and felt desperate and disabled since we were so far apart, and he was not due home until the next night.

The next few hours are a blur. I went to the First Step Program and had a shot for sexually transmitted diseases and took a large dose of medicines to prevent HIV, gonorrhea, chlamydia, and trichomonas. I answered question after question and tried my best to answer them, but my mind was a buzz. All I wanted to do was go home and hide in my closet and never come out. I was too traumatized to undergo a physical examination at this point and was told what to look for and if I had any concerns to contact them as soon as possible. I simply couldn't deal with someone, anyone, looking at my body or touching it in any way.

When my husband returned home, I picked him up at the airport. We held each other and cried a lot. He was incredibly angry, but his anger was not directed at me. He had actually phoned Johnathan and asked him to meet up with him, and, surprisingly, Johnathan agreed. His original intention was to notify the police of where Johnathan would be so it would be easy for them to pick him up and arrest him. But as any man who loves his wife and family would do, he wanted to kill Johnathan. He dropped me off and went to meet up with Johnathan in person. When he arrived at the place specified, he got out of the vehicle with a large wrench. He had him up against a wall cowering before him in a fetal position.

Before that night was out, my husband was spread eagle over the hood of a police car. It didn't end up in an arrest, since he never actually laid a hand on Johnathan. But the police did warn him to let them deal with this in their own way and time. To this day, he doesn't know why he didn't kill him. He struggled for months afterward with that question and went through months of counseling to come to grips with it. I am so grateful that he didn't kill Johnathan that day, and I believe it was the desperate prayers I was shooting up and asked my friends to shoot up after he left me to go meet up with Johnathan. God stopped him. If he had carried through, we would have had much more to go through than a rape trial, and I don't think we could have survived it as a family unit. It was already insurmountable what we had to deal with.

My husband and I have a very close relationship, and our family is extremely close. Everyone who knows us always comments on the closeness we have with each other. There was not a time when my husband or my kids blamed me or even hinted at blaming me for what happened. They understand my heart and my character and knew I had only tried to help Johnathan. But that didn't erase the betrayal and hurt that they were obviously dealing with too. Unless you walk through that same valley, it is nearly impossible to articulate how awful that feels.

That week, I noticed that my pelvic area was extremely sore. I dreaded going to the bathroom because when I needed to wipe the pressure from my hand resting against the pelvic bone hurt incredibly. I didn't know why it would hurt so much. Then I started to itch terribly in the private area, so I finally decided on Sunday that maybe I should go and have that exam after all to see what was going on. It turned out I was healing from bruises and lacerations from the blunt force trauma my body had undergone. The exam was horrid. It was invasive, painful, and embarrassing; and to top it off, it was recorded, and photos were taken. The itching, I was told, was from the abrasions healing and scabbing over, and my pelvic area was bruised. I was told that I would most likely feel more normal in a week to ten days. Although I was relieved at this news, I was incredibly angry at Johnathan for causing this pain to my body, let alone my soul.

My whole existence was flung into the abyss. I was devastated and felt incredibly lost. I didn't know how to go about doing life anymore. I didn't know who I was or what I was anymore. I couldn't find any peace or joy, and my smile was gone. I realized I was lost, and I had no idea of how to find my way back to my life as it was.

I cried continuously, and my skin was raw under my eyes from the constant flow of salt water. I didn't even bother to wear makeup. What was the point? I would only wash it off in a half an hour with my tears anyway.

Many people think that crimes like this are cut-and-dried. We watch on TV that a crime was committed and the bad guy is arrested right away and sent to jail where they belong. Let me tell you that crime in real life is far from that. There are many reasons someone is not immediately arrested as we found out. It took thirteen days before Johnathan was finally arrested. I would see him walking down the street and wished I could run him over with the car! His brother had informed me that Johnathan was planning on leaving the state, and I was in an absolute panic for the police to do something to stop him. I needed justice! I could not allow him to get away with all that he had done to me. He was originally arrested on the misdemeanor charges of violating the order of protection and immediately bonded out that day. The next day, he was supposed to go back to see the judge, and they rearrested him on a felony charge of attempted sexual intercourse without consent. His bail was set at $100,000, and that time he did not bond out.

The fact of the matter is that Johnathan raped me. The charge of "attempted" sexual intercourse without consent was a compromise on the part of the law enforcement and county attorney's office due to my statements upon the first questions asked of me. I was in a state of shock and confusion, and when asked about the details of where he placed himself in me, I was unsure of what they meant. I knew that Johnathan had not fully penetrated me, but I also knew that he was where he shouldn't be. He was very deliberate in what he was doing to me, watching me the entire time. I know my body but was ignorant of the terminology they used. So the question asked was, "Was his penis past the labia?" It was a huge question of confusion to me. Honestly, I think if they had given me a diagram and asked me to circle where he was, I would have been better off. But this is real life, and real life isn't like a TV show. This set the stage for much controversy down the road.

USlegal.com defines *penetration* in this way:

> *Laws* § 11-37-1(8), sexual *penetration* is *defined* as "sexual intercourse, cunnilingus, fellatio, and anal

intercourse, or any other intrusion, *however slight*, by any part of a person's body or by any object into the genital or anal openings of another person's body, but emission of semen is not required.""'

To the average person, like me, penetration meant the shaft of a male sex organ placed inside the woman's sex organ. I didn't know that there was a "legal" definition of this until I was the victim of a horrible crime. Although the detective was very kind and gentle in how he asked me this question, I was at a loss of how to answer it. I knew what had happened had happened, and that was all I could say. During this investigation, I was still in great distress, and it was a terrible place mentally, physically, and spiritually to have to revisit as much as I had to in order to give the authorities a good case to proceed with. I felt like a mental zombie.

I turned to the only place I knew to turn for my help. I cried out to God in the depth of my heart and asked him, no, literally begged him, to help me. I couldn't breathe from the weight of what I was forced to carry and the unbelievable hurt I felt inside. I found myself on the floor in my bedroom or on the bathroom floor, crying out to God to help me get up and take one more step. I knew how deeply I was hurting, and even worse was the obvious pain and disbelief my husband and son and daughter were going through. It ripped my heart out to see how much it affected them. No mother and no wife should ever have to see her family hurt so much or be so devastated. Still, through it all, we promised each other we would make it through this as a family and stay intact.

I spent a lot of my spare time on the Internet searching for assistance to help me understand and make sense of what I was going through. I knew I was in a dangerous place emotionally, and I sought help through the counseling available from the University of Montana SARC (Student Advocacy Resource Center) Program and through the YWCA. I went to both programs desperate to hold on to what little of me that was left and try to regain some of the power that I had lost in the attack. My point in telling about this aspect of my regaining my identity back is that I had to be proactive in everything I did and every avenue I went down to heal. I believe this must be the case for you or anyone else who has experienced something of this nature.

The fourth promise: "So do not fear, for I am with you; do not be dismayed, for I am your God. I will strengthen you and help you; I will uphold you with my righteous right hand" (Isaiah 41:10). God loves us so deeply. Even in the pit of despair and unbearable grief, he promises us that we do not need to be afraid or distressed about anything, because he is always with us. There are times when we are so secure in our relationship with Christ that we may become somewhat oblivious to his presence in our lives. Things may be going so smoothly that we don't consider the many ways Jesus reaches out to us in our daily lives. It could be a phone call, a note in the mail, an encouraging word, a smile, filling a need or fulfilling a desired wish, a scripture that we have read a thousand times before; but this time, it hits and pits our hearts. He will strengthen us and help us, upholding us with his righteous right hand. He will use all the things that are in our daily lives to reach out and assure us of his presence with us.

When we find ourselves in the darkest moments of our life, we have to look up to see the light. We have to focus on the promises of God to his children in order to get the courage to take the next breath. If you are a parent, there has probably been a time in your child's life that they were either terrified of the dark or the monster in the closet or the shadows on the walls. We calm them with our presence and soothe them with our words. We reach out and hold them until they can relax and fall asleep. God is that loving Father to us too, especially in the hardest moments of our lives. He calms us by his presence, he soothes us with his love letters to us, and he most definitely reaches out and holds us until we fall asleep. He *never* leaves our side, because he loves us that much. Having a clear understanding of the depth of his love is the foundation for which anyone can survive the unspeakable.

A bonus promise for this precious chapter: "I lift up my eyes to the mountains—where does my help come from? My help comes from the Lord, the maker of heaven and earth. He will not let your foot slip—he who watches over you will not slumber; indeed, he who watches over Israel will neither slumber nor sleep. The Lord watches over you—the Lord is your shade at your right hand" (Psalm 121:1–5).

In a visual image of the depth of the love directed at us by our compassionate heavenly Father, think about the famous poem "Footprints." When we are too weak and too tired to carry our burdens, He is there. When we don't have the strength or stamina to carry ourselves and we can't take one single step further, he carries us. He provides for us just as he provided for many of the characters we see in the Bible. Hagar, when she was abused by her mistress, fled into the wilderness. God comforted her, gave her sustenance, and sent her back to serve under Sarah. Hannah was given a son after many years of not conceiving a child. Naaman was cleansed from leprosy after dipping in the Jordan River seven times. Paul was rescued from the jail after being viciously beaten when people were praying unceasingly for him. Mary and Martha were grieving the death of their brother, Lazarus, when Jesus raised him from the dead. My point is that all these acts were acts of compassion and grace given to the servants of Christ. All came to him broken and hurt, and he knew all their pain already, and he carried them through the darkness into his healing light. He will carry you too. Trust. Release it and give it to him. You do not need to carry this burden alone. He is reaching down to you!

COME UP FOR AIR

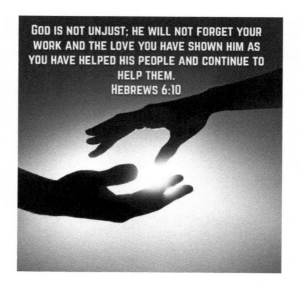

GOD IS NOT UNJUST; HE WILL NOT FORGET YOUR WORK AND THE LOVE YOU HAVE SHOWN HIM AS YOU HAVE HELPED HIS PEOPLE AND CONTINUE TO HELP THEM.
HEBREWS 6:10

I sat across from my friend drinking a coffee and eating oatmeal with fruit in it. She had just shared a very personal experience with me in an effort to connect with me in the cavernous pit I was in. She had known me for several years. We had gone to church together and spent time together in social settings. Our families had laughed and celebrated a lot together. I had held and cherished her babies. She knew all about the depth of the help I had given to Johnathan and all the work I had done in the homeless sector of our community. I was crying again. "Are you *grieving*?" The question stunned me. She was incredulous. Was I grieving? Was I *grieving*? Of course, I was grieving! What kind of a question was that? When I answered her question, she followed it up with, "Why?" She simply could not understand why I would feel such loss.

Well, let's see. How about the end of my purity with my husband of twenty-five years? Granted, I never gave Johnathan what he took, but I was no longer able to say I hadn't been touched by another man since our wedding vows. In my mind, I was damaged goods, marred, ugly, and dirty. Yes, I was grieving. Grieving because Johnathan had broken my heart with his behavior and stripped me of my identity. I felt unworthy of my husband, my kids, my friends, my church, my God. Every aspect of my life was affected by this. Yes, I was grieving!

It seemed that no matter where I went or whom I talked to, I was met with that same kind of mentality, or, worse, I was blamed for what had happened to me, or, at the very least, I felt the doubt come across in nonverbal ways. Questions like, "Well, why *did* you go down there? Did you fight? Did you scream? Why not?" Those are all questions that take the blame off the one whom it belongs to and transplants it to the one who was assaulted. It is called rape culture. It takes a horrible tragedy like this to find out who your real support system is and who will actually dare to sit with you in the ashes and comfort you.

"I would have fought! I would have screamed! I would had kicked him in the groin! I would have scratched his eyeballs out. I would have done this. I would have done that. I would have never gone down there in the first place." I was told many times I should take self-defense courses. I was told I should get a concealed weapon permit and carry a gun. At the very least, I should carry a rape whistle and mace.

I would be amiss if I didn't mention the ones who didn't know how to respond to me, so they simply ignored my existence and my pain. Rather than try to comfort me, they avoided me like the plague and quit talking to me or looking me in the eyes. These ones hurt me the most. I was okay before, when someone hadn't cut me deep in my soul, but now I was like a leper. I sometimes felt like if they dared to communicate with me, they thought they would somehow get what I had, like a communicable disease. If they breathed the same air around me, would they be afflicted too?

I have come to realize that rape culture exists because people like me don't speak out about their experiences. We don't stand up and demand change. We are so traumatized by the experience we are terrified to talk about it for fear of judgment. "Slut shaming" is another phrase that I read about a lot. What did *she* do to bring this on herself? Was she dressed immodestly? Was she drinking? Was she at a party? Was she doing drugs? Was she flirting? Did she talk to the person who raped her? Why was she alone with him? Rape culture is a mind-set of ignoring the incident, making it look less traumatic than it was, explaining it away in some way that excuses the behavior of the perpetrator, laughing it away with jokes or various other degree of denial. Rape culture is wrong.

Let's get something straight. If you were raped, *it is not your fault*. We live in a fallen world where people do not allow Jesus to sit on the throne of their hearts. This is a sin that was committed against you. Blame does not belong to you, so don't own that, and don't allow people to make you wear blame like a necklace around your neck. The chains of depression, despair, and grief can keep you locked in a prison. You may feel like you will never escape this shame, but God will come through for you. The biggest lie you can believe is that you are the reason this happened. This is *not* your shame; it is your rapist's and only your rapist's.

Ann sat across from me in her office and looked at me with genuine compassion and concern. "I can see that your perception of the world has been shattered. Barb, this is *not* your fault. I know you feel that way, but it isn't your fault. Let's talk about why you feel that way." I thought about her inquiry. Why *did* I feel that way? I had spent a bunch of time with Johnathan in the past. I enjoyed being with him. I had thought of him as a friend. I told him many times I knew he would never hurt me. I believed I was truly making a difference to him. I didn't run away. I froze. It was not the first time he assaulted me. I knew what he could be like. I was too trusting. I was too naive. I was the one who was "normal" in the mind. I have so much shame. I am the one who sought him out that day. I was so convinced he needed to hear my words from me. I was publicly raped and humiliated . . . I was unable to stop myself from sobbing.

Ann was kind and just let me cry. She knew it had to come out. She knew I was in a very delicate emotional place and was teetering on the brink of taking my life.

This was my first meeting with the University of Montana SARC (Student Advocacy Resource Center) program. Although I was not a student, I was allowed to take advantage of the free counseling. Ann was a gentle Native American intern at the branch of the Curry Health Center. I was so desperate for help and validation as a human being that I asked them if I could see someone as soon as possible.

The YWCA didn't initially want to see me as a regular appointment with someone since I had been there previously for the assault in January of the same year. They offered walk-in appointments at certain times of the day during the week, but I couldn't make those work; plus I felt I needed to have someone to talk to consistently rather than talking to several people in bits and pieces. Later on, they determined since it was a new assault and a much more violent one, they could counsel me. Now, however, I was considered an "Emergency," so they agreed to let me go through the services offered at the university.

One of the hardest merry-go-rounds to get off is the self-blaming, self-abasing one. I was filled with misplaced guilt for what had happened to me. It took a lot of work to get past that. I spent hours and hours absorbing what I could find on the Internet. I went to Christian sights trying to find God in this pain. I went to legal websites seeking information on what might come next. I went to suicide prevention sights looking for a way to tie a knot and hold on just one more second. I reached out to my closest friends who let me cry on their shoulders and carried my pain with me. I sought out topical Bible studies on rape and forgiveness. But I didn't go to my family outside of my husband, son, or daughter. I was too ashamed of what I was going through, and I was sure I would be judged. As it turns out, I was right on some levels. However, to my relief, most of my family on both sides were surprisingly supportive and helpful to us. Having a dedicated support system is imperative to healing. As I said earlier, you will find out who will and will not be there for you in the hardest storms of life. There will be some surprises along the way if you keep your eyes open. Those you just know will be there for you will suddenly be gone. And those you don't think will be there with you will be the ones who stay by your side until you make it through the valley and back onto the mountaintop where you can breathe clean refreshing air again.

One resounding truth I read repeatedly was this: "You did not deserve this, and you *will* survive this." PTSD, anxiety, and depression go hand in hand when someone has been raped. The self-image of the woman (or man) who has been raped can be torn to shreds. It may seem like you are damaged goods, dirty, or disgusting.

Relationships can feel uncertain at best and dangerous at most. You may not trust your judgment for a while when it comes to people. You may be too afraid to do your normal activities. But take heart. This is all *normal*. When I read those words for the first time, I was so relieved to know that what I was feeling was totally normal and I wasn't losing my mind. Be gentle with yourself. Be mindful of the work you need to do to help yourself, and, above all else, give yourself time.

"I don't normally give my clients this book so early in the recovery process, but something tells me that you would really benefit from this." Ann handed me a book entitled *The Rape Survival Handbook*. Just the title sent shivers down my spine, but I accepted it gratefully. That book and Ann truly were my lifeline. I was desperate to make the rubble of my life into some semblance of "normal." I needed the words in that book. They were healing balm that would start me on the road to recovery.

"Barb, I know this is going to be hard for you, but I want to challenge you to write a letter to your traumatized self. Address it to your victim self. I want you to write exactly how you feel, and don't hold back, no matter what comes out. Just write. And then after a day or two, I want you to write a letter back to yourself. But, this time, I want you to try and write it from the viewpoint of someone you are trying to comfort. How would you talk to your best friend if this happened to her? Would you judge her? Or would you tell her it isn't her fault?"

Writing the first letter to myself was surprisingly easy. I was so full of self-blame, condemnation, and self-hate that the words sprang onto the page. It's pretty shocking to me now when I reread those words.

> Dear Barb, (Victim)
>
> Why did you go down there anyway! You are so incredibly stupid! You deserve what you got! You knew that he could be dangerous. He had already demonstrated that to you. What were you thinking you stupid, stupid, stupid idiot! Because of you, your family is disgraced. You are a selfish, self-centered wimp! Who do you think you are? Why do you insist in the belief that good exists in all people? How many times do you need to put yourself in a position where something bad can happen? You have no right to feel sorry for yourself. People will look at you and see you for the disgusting piece of garbage that you are. You are nothing! Go crawl in a hole and don't show your face. You have nothing in you that can ever be beautiful, nothing that can ever be useful again. You suck. You have ruined your marriage and your husband will never see you as pure again. Why didn't you fight? Why didn't you scream? You saw those people walking by so why didn't you call for help? You gave him the idea that you wanted him because you showed up down there. You make me sick. And you bring shame on the name of Jesus. How dare you think he could care to help you? You deserve this.
>
> *Barbie*

I felt the utter hate seeping through every pore of my being when I wrote those words. I believed the lies that Satan was whispering in my ears day and night. My identity was tied to helping the helpless and now my identity was in crisis. The response letter was much harder to write, but I must admit, it did some good. I will tell you why in a bit.

> Dear Barbie, (Survivor)
>
> I understand your anger at me. But I also know your true heart. This took place in broad daylight. You were a victim, not the perpetrator. There were people all around you. How could you have known that he would do that to you? He's sick, Barb. You didn't understand the look on his face or in his eyes. He made his mind up he was going to do this to you. I'm convinced he would have done this sooner or later, even if you had not gone down there to talk to him. I'm also very upset that you froze when he did this. This is your natural defense mechanism. It isn't a choice you made. But, remember you begged him to stop. You begged him to think about what he was doing. He pinned you up against that log. If you had fought him, you may not be here today. I'm sorry you feel you let yourself down. I'm sorry you feel you let our family down. I'm sorry you made a poor choice, but you are not to blame for what he did to you! He owns that and he needs to live with it. As far as deserving what you got, that is a lie from Satan. Nobody ever deserves to be hurt this way. And God knows what happened that day and all the others. He knows you are innocent. I know you are angry, and I know you are hurting. But you are still loved. Your friends all know your true character. You need to hold onto that. I still love you.
>
> Barb

I owed it to myself to try to help myself heal because I was still a good person. I deserved to be happy just as much as anyone did, and I needed to feel whole again. I needed to learn to set safe boundaries for myself in my healing process, so I created a contract to myself. I promised myself I would listen to the inner warnings that I was pushing too hard, but yet I would give ear to my heart cries by journaling and letting them out. I promised myself to not judge my efforts as not good enough or to berate myself if I had a tough time sticking to my contract. I promised myself that I would hold back from sharing my thoughts and writings with others or even thinking about certain events or emotions if the territory didn't feel completely safe to do so. I promised myself I wouldn't work on things if I was too stressed out, too tired, too hungry, or otherwise sick from an illness or if anyone in my immediately family was sick from an illness. Lastly, I promised myself that I wouldn't work on these things at all if I couldn't have someone to talk to and help me to sort through things that might come up. That is where Ann and the YWCA came in.

One thing I learned from the YWCA was to change the channel. You may ask what that means. I am not talking about the TV, but the channel in my brain that was continuing to relive the horrible traumatic event in its entirety. When these most troublesome times were on rerun in my head, usually at three thirty in the morning, I would have to concentrate very hard on switching the channel in my brain to think of something else. It could be a place that I have been before where I felt happy, safe, and warm. For me, it was Jamaica on my honeymoon with my husband. I would think about the waterfall in Ocho Rios that we climbed. I would imagine how the rocks felt while we were walking up the waterfall, amazed at the lack of moss on them. The water was warm, yet the rush and force of the waterfall behind us was loud and exciting. The air was sultry with the mist of the rainforest, and the colors were vibrant and inviting. That was my favorite channel to change my mind to. I would think of the love my husband, and I shared and the security I felt back then. I would hold onto that and bring it to the present.

This was not an easy task, but it did work wonders for me. Each time my mind would wander back to the events that held me hostage, I would force myself to change the channel back again. I had to decide what I would let my mind dwell on to break that cycle of trauma. Sometimes, I would change the channel to my children and their births and achievements in the years I have been blessed to be with them. Sometimes, I would change the channel and think of songs I loved to sing. In my case, most the music I listened to is Christian, so I would always have a verse on my heart to think about. On other occasions, I would change the channel and think of particularly encouraging Bible verses that God would give to me—morsels that gave me strength and comfort and encouragement when I needed them most.

As I mentioned earlier, writing the response letter to myself actually did do some good. Ann was so right when she asked me about how I would treat my best friend if this has happened to her instead of to me. I would have been right by her side through the thick and thin no matter what. I would tell her she was loved, beautiful, and precious in the sight of the Lord. I would tell her that the person who attacked her was a horrible person battling with demons that we can't understand. I would pray with her and hold her. So that letter written to myself was the first step toward loving myself again.

At the time of my rape, I was a size 8. As I write this book, I am a size 14. I was asked recently if I just don't feel I deserve to be beautiful anymore. It crushed my spirit to have that judgmental question asked to me. It comes from a perspective of one who obviously doesn't understand that trauma affects all aspects of your life. People react one of two ways: they either gain weight, or they lose it. Rarely do they stay the same. It isn't that we wake up one day and say to ourselves, "Hey, let's make yourself fat. That would be a great idea, don't you think?" It solidified the very things I have written about regarding rape culture and the misguided attitudes and comments of well-meaning people. Although her words cut me, I do not harbor anger at her, because I know her heart and I know she didn't mean to come across that way. Guaranteed, she has no clue she even affected me adversely. We walk through a valley of trauma, but that doesn't mean we will stay there forever. The trip backs up to the mountain-top takes time, just as our healing will take time.

I am reminded of the story of Tamar in the Bible. She was raped by her brother Amnon. He made himself sick by being obsessed with Tamar. His advisor Jonadab told him to pretend to be sick and ask the king for Tamar to come and prepare a meal for him and feed it to him. So she does. He is filled with lust for his half sister and forces himself on her. Tamar used her voice to try and reason with him, even telling him that the king would give her to him in marriage if he asked. *"No, my brother, do not force me; for such a thing is not done in Israel; do not do anything so vile! As for me, where could I carry my shame? And as for you, you would be as one of the scoundrels in Israel. Now therefore, I beg you, speak to the king; for he will not withhold me from you."* He would have no part of it. Afterward, he hated her with an intense hate, even more than how much he loved her, and he drove her out. She tore her robe and put ashes on her head. She left weeping loudly. Her brother Absalom took her in. Eventually, Absalom killed Amnon to vindicate the disgrace on his sister Tamar. In a lot of ways, I am Tamar embodied. I cared for the needs of a sick man, and he twisted it and forced himself on me, using his body to trap me just as Amnon used his to trap Tamar. I tried to use my voice to stop him, and he would have none of it. The account is found in 2 Samuel 13.

I mention this particular story because although it didn't happen right away, it is clear that the sin of Amnon against his sister was not lost on God. The king, King David, did not do anything to Amnon after he disgraced his sister. Perhaps Absalom waited for his father, the king, to say or do something, *anything* to address it; but he didn't. So, therefore, Absalom finally took matters into his own hands two years later and had him killed. Although I am not condoning murder here, I am simply stating that it was not lost on God. He knew about it too and allowed the death of Amnon.

I clearly remember reading about this account in the first couple of months after Johnathan had raped me. I found it to be extremely sad, yet comforting at the same time. I knew while reading this that God was telling me that he was not minimizing my disgrace and that he was already working on my behalf to lift my head once again. Tamar's story offers hope, healing, love, and justice. She didn't go quietly away and pretend this didn't happen to her. She tore her robe, put ashes on her head, and wailed loudly, proclaiming in the streets the guilt of her attacker. With her actions, she bravely indicted her half brother and exposed him for the evil he had committed.

The fifth promise: "He will wipe every tear from their eyes, and there will be no more death or sorrow or crying or pain. All these things are gone forever. All our pain, depression, anxiety, tears, hurt, and every sad day we experience will disappear forever" (Revelation 21:4).

Forever. Crying will cease. Suffering will not exist, and we will live in perfect harmony and peace with our Creator! What an incredibly encouraging thought. Yes, our hurt and our depression will end someday. But it doesn't have to be tomorrow. This is a painful season, but it will end. It may be long, or it may be short, or it may be a lifetime battle, but each day we live, we can practice living forward, being hopeful of what is to come. Our lives here are such a miniscule moment compared to eternity. We can choose to be hopeful. We can be joyful in hope, patient in affliction, and faithful in prayer (Romans 12:12). God is honored in our hope and trust in him. Many times over, I heard how much my faith was an encouragement to others because I didn't give up on God. He was and is good! He is a good, good Father. I am loved by him; that's who I am. Who are you? Regardless of your faith in him, you are loved by him. That's who you are.

YOU'RE SO STRONG

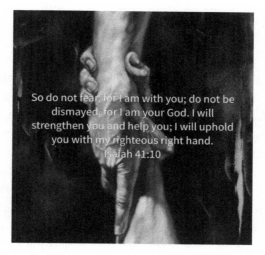

So do not fear, for I am with you; do not be dismayed,
for I am your God. I will strengthen you and help you;
I will uphold you with my righteous right hand.

—Isaiah 41:10

To quote my daughter, "Some days I just can't human." Over the course of the year leading up to the trial, this sentiment really did match me. There were days when I really wanted to run away or just walk away from this whole ugly ordeal. And there were also way too many days when I seriously contemplated suicide. I did not want to go through this and prayed continuously that God would cause Johnathan to finally just admit what he did. I wanted to give up and go away and lick my wounds like a wounded animal would. But I didn't. Why? Because the Lord didn't want me to. He assured me that he was going to use this ugly and painful situation to his glory.

I am reminded of a particular day that I recorded my thoughts. At least three times that day, I heard these words from three various sources. They were the following:

1) I am defined by God's love for me, not my circumstances.
2) Jesus is here with me, and he will not leave me. He is and will continue to fight for me; this battle is his.
3) My insecurities don't define who I am.
4) I am not useless.

"When you pass through the waters, I will be with you; and through the rivers, they shall not overwhelm you; when you walk through fire you shall not be burned, and the flame shall not consume you" (Isaiah 43:2). And at least a dozen times that week alone, I heard, "Cast your burdens on him because he cares for you." So now I ask you, if the God of the universe loves me enough to reinforce me that much, shouldn't I love him enough to take him at his word? What if I told you that he loves *you* that much too? When we don't have enough strength to pick ourselves up off the ground, dust ourselves off, and move on, I guarantee he *does*! The wonderful thing about our heavenly Dad is that we don't even have to reach up to him, because he is already reaching down to us, offering his hand so he can pull us up. And if we cry, it is okay! *It really is okay.* The Lord is our comfort, and his strength is made perfect in our weakness. Our love is imperfect. But his love is perfect! Can you imagine what a miserable existence this would be without him?

I have learned that when God decides to use you, he will use something bigger than you to do it. This rape—this trial, every aspect of it—was and still is bigger than me. Even so, I have heard repeated to me in so many ways and places by so many people, "You are so strong." I must admit I came to somewhat dread those words because I felt far from strong. I felt weak, scared, shamed, and ugly. But I was not viewed that way by those who really know me and love me. The weak, scared, shamed, and ugly Barbie Jenkins was the one the devil was constantly tormenting with thoughts of self-blame, hate, suicide, and all sorts of negative thoughts. But God's voice was bigger, louder, stronger, and more consistent; and I chose to listen to his voice. In that sense then, yes, I was so strong.

I gather my strength largely from music. I listen to Christian radio all the time, and when I am not listening to the radio, I am listening to the music I have stored in iTunes. Christian music is lathered in Bible verses, encouragement, and love. It was simply amazing to me when I was driving down the road praying, crying, and praying some more when a song would come on the radio and speak right directly to my heart.

David Crowder sings a song he wrote called "I Am." This was an example of how God used music to speak to me. The song talks about how there is no place we can go that God isn't able to be with us and how there is no situation that we can't find peace in because of him. The chorus says I am holding on to you in the middle of the storm. I took this song literally. In the Bible, God is referred to as I Am. Every time I felt absolutely unable to go another second, it seems that song would come on the radio, and I would hear those words, "I Am holding on to you." Not only was I holding on to him, but the Great I Am was holding on to me! He would wake me in the morning, and I would have this song cascading through my brain. I was 100 percent dependent on the Lord to help me through each and every second.

I was devastated when I couldn't sing. I used to sing on the praise team every Sunday at our small church Echo Missoula. I sat in the back of the room and cried during worship for the first six weeks. I couldn't sing. I couldn't even bring myself to sit with the group. I was so ashamed of what I was going through, and I felt so unworthy to be in the midst of other Christians. My heart was totally broken, and I really did lose my song temporarily. I would sit and cry silently, and sometimes a sob would escape me, but mostly I just sat and listened with my heart to the soothing words of love and encouragement my church was singing. Sometimes, I would have silent tears streaming down my face; and my sisters would come and sit with me, not saying anything but just bearing that pain with me, holding my hand or letting me lean my head on their shoulder.

One day while I was sitting at home alone, I was struck with the need to express my brokenness to the Lord in song. It wasn't just any song, but a very specific song. "Abba Father." The word *abba* in Aramaic means "father," but it isn't just the common word for *father*. It indicates a very close, intimate relationship of the father to his child and the childlike trust the child has for his father. I can call on God as Abba because I am his child. I came as a daughter and sang these words to my father:

In the garden where our Savior prayed, our salvation was secured, as He prayed, "Not my will but Thine be done." Who can know the torments of the cross where his grace and love outpoured. The suffering servant is God's only Son. "Abba Father, Lord God Almighty. Holy, Father, we give you glory." And in our darkest moments, with shadows closing in, the Spirit helps his family to pray. He gives us understanding. He helps us in our need. He gives us the ability to say, "Abba Father, Lord God Almighty. Holy Father, we give you glory" (by Maranatha Singers).

As I was down on my knees, I sang from the broken bottom of my heart to Abba Father. I had tears streaming down my face as I put myself in the presence of the most Holy God. He restored my voice that day and broke the barrier down in my inability to sing. He swept his spirit over me, and I have never felt more close or secure in my relationship with Christ as I did that day. From that day forward, I was able to sing again at our services at Echo, although I took a couple months before getting up again with the praise team. I still struggled with my unworthiness to help lead worship for months after that, but with the encouragement from my family and friends, I was back up front again, singing songs of praise to God. And, yes, I cried a lot. I would look out in the crowd and see my Christian family looking up at me and smiling to encourage me. I didn't feel judged when I had tears coming down my face. I was healing. I was finding strength. Strength was being supplied to me and then multiplied. Much as a single cell is multiplied to become a human being, my "spirit cells" were multiplying.

Learning to navigate life in trauma mode was excruciating. That is why moments like what I just described were so invaluable to me. I was trying to balance "normalcy" with multiple interruptions of going to the police department to work with the kind detective assigned to me and my case to the county attorney's office and multiple counseling sessions per week and still do work and family life.

Suzy Boylan was the lead county attorney assigned to this case, and she worked closely with Brian Lowney, who assisted her the whole time. Brian was my first point of contact as Suzy was out of town when the case came to them. When I met Suzy, I was struck by how tiny and beautiful she was. Once we started to work together, I was pleased at how much of a giant she could be. She was strong and supportive and kind. She was prepared and matter-of-fact and was not afraid to pull punches and ask the tough questions, but she never gave me the impression that she for an instant doubted my story. She is a tiny bag of dynamite, and I was thankful to have her on my side!

Brian called me on the phone and tried to prepare me for what might happen in the newspapers. Brian was a quiet but sincere man. He could be firm one moment, then throw you off with a comment that would make you burst into laughter. I really appreciated his presence throughout the entire process. I had already been traumatized even more by the inappropriate and inaccurate information given to the newspaper by the police, and Brian was completely aware of this fact. The article in question that came out in the paper was horrendous. It gave way too much information about me and was also embellishing the account as if what happened wasn't horrible enough. It forced me and my husband to tell our children, our employers, and our church family what had happened before we had a chance to think of how and when we could convey what we needed to. It added to my disgrace and compounded my pain.

Suzy was extremely thorough and incredibly sensitive to my fragile state. She was patient and kind and reassuring to my husband and me. She did an excellent job preparing me for the trial and made herself available to me whenever I needed to talk to her. She spent countless hours with me, especially asking questions and putting together her case against Johnathan. My advocate Erin was always there by my side as well and was a wealth of encouragement and support to me. Between these two women, I had a wonderful system of communication.

To be sure, the entire process was incredibly hard to go through. I have been asked by many various sources if I would encourage others to report their rapes based on my experience. I always have to say yes. Not because of the outcome but because I firmly believe that if more of us would speak up and stand up against our attackers, things might change for the future of victims.

One of the most emotionally draining events leading up to the trial was my "interview" with the defense attorneys. I was told it would only be a couple of hours maximum. The length of this meeting surprised even Suzy, Brian, and Erin, who were there to support me. The "interview" was more like an interrogation where the defense could say whatever they wanted to say and behave however they wanted to behave without the safety net of a judge present to keep them in line. I also was not allowed to have any of my family with me for support. Suzy and Brian both warned me that this would be a draining experience, but even so, I was not prepared for how vicious these two women would be to me. I was in the conference room for over five hours with relentless accusations and questions regarding my relationship with Johnathan. I sat while being sneered at by both of them the entire time. I knew going into it that the prosecution team would mostly be silent while listening for the defense to show their cards and give clues of how they might proceed with the trial.

It was clear that they were going to go after me and try to paint me as a lovesick woman with some confused and conflicted feelings toward Johnathan. The line of questioning was incredibly offensive and insensitive. Questions like, "Where were your hands? Where were you sitting? Did you 'help' others too? Where did you get the coffee you brought him? How often did you do that? Did you bring others coffee? Did you claim your charity on your taxes? I want a copy of your taxes. Did you provide all your e-mails to the county? Did the mission know of your 'help' to Johnathan?" These were asked multiple times with sarcasm and judgment dripping off every word. It was geared to undermine my truth and rattle me.

At one point, I had to ask for a break. I was really unnerved and emotionally exhausted. Suzy, Brian, and Erin took me back to Suzy's office and talked me through the emotions I was having. I had a good cry, then took a deep breath and went back to face whom I now considered to be the twin daughters of Satan. When I went back into that room, I was more determined than ever to push back and not allow them to try and paint me as someone I knew I wasn't. I looked them straight in their hate-filled eyes and answered every question they threw at me truthfully and repeatedly. Finally, the interrogation was over, and I could leave but not without being told I would provide x, y, and z to them. I refused when it came to my taxes. I told them they could never prove how much of my charity was to Johnathan or other people, as I really did do a lot for many different people. Besides that, I felt it was none of their business. If they wanted that, then they would have to subpoena me. After that, they dropped that subject.

The common consensus after that meeting, from Suzy, Brian, and Erin's viewpoints, was that they had never seen anyone be treated the way I was treated in that interview. They were shocked with the tactics of the defense attorneys and the constant sneering that was directed at me with the sarcasm in each statement or question. I was left wondering how a woman can defend a male rapist and so unabashedly attack the victim as they were attacking me. I knew at that moment that this was going to be the platform to which I could expect to be treated in court. The only difference is that with a jury and the judge there, they would be forced to temper their sneers and sarcastic comments in order to not make themselves look unfavorable to the jury or be reprimanded by the judge. I also realized in a hurry that Johnathan had all the rights here, and I had very few. Because the state had the burden of proof, the rights of Johnathan were placed above mine as his victim.

In the meantime, I had started counseling with a professional counselor named Rob Terwilliger. My initial trepidation about having a male counselor was quickly eased. Rob was very sensitive to my trauma and the deep level of PTSD I was suffering with. He asked me questions and listened intently to my answers, not judging me or causing me to feel like I was a bad person for what had happened to me.

Rob was extremely instrumental in helping me to find ways to ground myself. Early on, I had to point out to him that having his red coat in the room hanging on the back of his chair was a major trigger to me. This is because Johnathan almost never went without his red coat, and my brain equated red coats to him. Even now, I still have to tell myself it is okay when I see a man in a red coat. It seems like an unreasonable fear, but it is all part of the trauma and PTSD I was and still am suffering with, so, therefore, it was really quite "normal" given my situation. Being sensitive to this, Rob was careful not to have his red coat in the room while I was there.

When I would suffer with flashbacks, which was extremely often, Rob taught me to look around and physically touch something and verbally say what that object was. He would ask me questions like, "What does that feel like? Is it soft, hard, cold, hot, sharp, dull, smooth, etc. He said that doing that would reinforce to my brain that I was present and not in the midst of the traumatic scene where I was raped. So I used this technique quite often. Sometimes the objects were inanimate, and sometimes they were not.

Rob was also supergood about reinforcing the fact that I was not to blame for what happened to me. He was excellent about reframing things and giving me another way to perceive it. An example of this was that I felt incredibly judgmental of myself because I didn't fight. Rob said, "But you *did* fight. You tried to stop him with your words. You tried to get out of there. Remember that you were on crutches! You were unable to put weight down on your foot, and he knew that. You didn't just allow him to do this to you. Afterward, you confronted him and told him he was responsible for this and not you. You did what you could do." Then he would remind me that when your body goes into freeze mode, it is your brain's way of protecting you from the trauma that your body is experiencing. That is why I didn't immediately feel the pain that Johnathan had inflicted on my body. All the cortisone rush that my body produced was to protect me. My body produced so much so quickly that it took time to release it, and once it started to release it, then I could feel the pain.

Rob also worked at length with me on breathing exercises that were geared to help me calm myself. He would do mindfulness meditations with me and guide me to take notice of each area of my body and how to breathe through the tension and release it. These were incredibly beneficial to me, and I used them often throughout the day when I could feel myself getting into a negative mind frame and in the middle of the night when I just couldn't sleep.

One way of calming myself with this breathing was to simultaneously hug myself, patting one arm then the next while deep breathing. I bet it may have looked like I was crazy, but the end result was very favorable, so I was okay with looking a little foolish. I figured nobody else could get me through this but me and God who was providing me with all these avenues to healing. He was placing all these people and things in my life, but I had to do my part too. I had to utilize them.

The greatest tool Rob used with me is called EMDR Therapy. It is specially geared to reduce anxiety and depression associated with PTSD. I was suffering acutely with this condition because of this attack. I had numerous triggers and constant flashbacks and recurring nightmares. I was exhausted from the stress and depression and wondered if I would ever be able to live my life as a "normal" woman again. I feared this was my forever reality.

My advocate Erin is the one who first broached the subject of EMDR Therapy with me. She sent me an e-mail with a link that had all sorts of information about it and how it worked. Suzy was the next one to mention it to me, and one of the women from the YWCA mentioned it as well. EMDR was relatively new and known as the most highly effective treatment used in treating soldiers with PTSD. The success rate was phenomenal, and the time frame to a more neutral existence was relatively short when compared to your traditional methods of treating PTSD via medicine or regular counseling.

EMDR stands for Eye Movement Desensitization and Reprocessing. How it normally works is with the counselor having you watch his finger going with a rhythm back and forth and you following it while listening to a beeping sound at the same pace. This is done in short successions. While this is going on, the patient will revisit the traumatic event and all the emotions associated with it, then talk about them briefly with the counselor, then do another round starting where they left off before. The idea is that each time the patient "goes there" in his or her mind, the external stimuli are keeping them present and reminding them that they are safe.

For me, Rob used an adaptation of the version I described above. Mostly because my eyes do not work together due to an illness when I was a baby leaving me blind. I have one very dominant eye, and the other doesn't really see. So, for me, I wore headphones, which I would hear the beeping in, but I also had "clickers" in my hands that would vibrate along with the beeping in my ears. So the right clicker would vibrate at the same time the beep would sound in my right ear, then the left and back to the right and so on.

For me, EMDR was a godsend. I was allowed to really go back in thirty-second intervals and search my memories and take note of all my senses at the time. I could remember a lot of details that had gotten muddled in my traumatized brain. Once I was able to do this and talk about these disturbing facts and sort things out with Rob, my PTSD simmered to a soft boil. I could function in less acute trauma and deal with the depression and begin to find the road back to my life. I now had a willingness to survive. EMDR helped me with the past, the present, and my future. I highly recommend this if you are struggling with PTSD.

The sixth promise: "A bruised reed he will not break, and a smoldering wick he will not snuff out. In faithfulness he will bring forth justice" (Isaiah 42:3). I do believe that the God of the heavens is so incredibly compassionate to us. Maybe more than we can possibly imagine. And that compassion that he directs at us in our time of deep despair can't be compared to anything else! I love that the Lord doesn't ever leave us and how he loves us so much that he takes care to keep our lights shining. Have you ever seen a lantern or a candle when there is a breeze or wind, but it keeps on burning in the wind? Well, when we have hurricanes and tsunamis and tornadoes raging in our spiritual lives, God places his covering over us and protects our light so it doesn't get snuffed out. The key is to turn to him and depend on him and his steadfast love and support. It is an honor to me when he allows me to glimpse just how long, how wide, how high, and how deep his love is for us. Praise him in the storm, and never stop! He loves your praise as much as he loves you.

THE WOMAN IN THE MIRROR

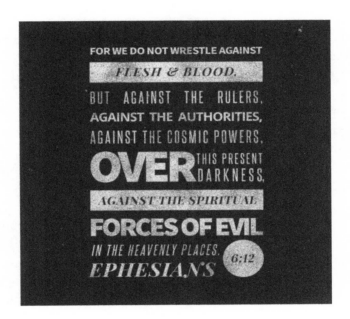

FOR WE DO NOT WRESTLE AGAINST *FLESH & BLOOD,* BUT AGAINST THE RULERS, AGAINST THE AUTHORITIES, AGAINST THE COSMIC POWERS, **OVER** THIS PRESENT DARKNESS, *AGAINST THE SPIRITUAL* **FORCES OF EVIL** IN THE HEAVENLY PLACES. *EPHESIANS* 6:12

Have you ever looked at yourself in the mirror and intently just considered your eyes? I have. A person's eyes tell so much about them. I spend a lot of time actually looking into people's eyes. Sometimes it is amazing what I see, sometimes it is sweet what I see, sometimes is sad what I see, and other times it downright scares me what I see. Some people have mastered the art of deception and are good at hiding what is inside. I am not one of those people. You pretty much can tell by looking at me how I am really doing. I am who I am, and you get what you see. You have probably heard it said that the eyes are the windows to the soul. My husband used to call me "Awesome Eyes" because my eyes change color based on my moods and what I am wearing. But he has always been able to read my mood by my eyes, and I have never been able to hide that from him or anyone. No matter how I tried, I could not mask the pain in my soul.

For me, looking in the mirror after this attack caused me a great deal of distress. I hated to see the wounded spirit looking out those windows at me. I missed the shining, happy spirit that used to be there. I mourned for who I once was and wondered if I would ever get any part of that back or if I was stuck here forever. I hated that when people looked at me, they were mourning for the me that I was too. She was gone. I had to face that fact and embrace the me that was here, and so did everyone else around me.

After a particularly bad night, I would try to get ready in the morning and prepare myself so I didn't look so haggard. It was super-hard. I now had bags under my eyes that didn't use to be there, and I looked tired and dead inside. It matched how I felt inside. I was flat. No spark, no spunk, just going through the motions, and to top it off, I was gaining weight. Now I not only felt ugly on the inside, but I felt ugly on the outside too. No amount of makeup, no new clothes, no different hairstyles could make me feel any better about myself.

My husband was experiencing this same phenomenon. He struggled each day too and was unable to look at himself in the mirror. He carried his own weight of self-blame for what had happened to me. If he had said this or done that, this wouldn't have happened. If he hadn't been out of town, this wouldn't have happened. If he had confronted Johnathan forcefully, this wouldn't have happened. The list went on and on. It was fruitless for either of us to entertain these thoughts, but, nonetheless, it is where he was at in processing the whole painful truth of what we were enduring. The reality is that Johnathan chose what he did to me, and if it hadn't been that day, it would have been another. I am certain of this fact.

We had ten and a half months between the date of the rape to the date that the trial finally begun. The trial was originally scheduled for April 2016, but then it was postponed by the defense attorneys. Our new date was now scheduled for Wednesday, August 31. Trial was expected to last approximately three days. It lasted six instead, over a period of two weeks!

In preparation for this event, our church rallied around us. I asked my friend Ann Marie if we could borrow their place for a gathering. I wanted to surround myself and my family with our Christian brothers and sisters. I asked if it would be okay to have anyone that could meet with us on that Tuesday before the trial. I wanted to spend time in prayer and song and worship. She and her husband, Brett were incredibly gracious about this and readily agreed. My husband's brother and his wife were in town to support us too, so they came along as well. Another brother was in the air from Atlanta to attend the trial with us, or he would have been there as well. I had church members, friends, neighbors, and even a lady from my rape support group there. My best friend here, Liz, had some horrible things going on in her own life, but even she took the time to come to this special evening. We had somewhere around forty to forty-five people there at Ann Marie's home. This show of support was incredible to me and touched me deeply. I also invited Suzy, Brian, Erin, and Rob to this event. It was a good opportunity to have Suzy and Brian address my friends.

Because of the monumental purpose of this meeting, I had let people all over the country know of our meeting time. I asked them all to please consider gathering together with other Christians to offer praise and prayer on our behalf to God at the same time, only in their own time zones. I had prayer warriors all over the place praying with us that night. I wanted to make sure that my armor, and that of our family, was securely in place. I am a firm believer in the power of prayer, and God promises to us that where two or more are gathered in his name, there he is also. I knew my friends were coming through for us in this horrible time of our lives, and my heart was overwhelmed with gratefulness to them all.

One of the most distressing things about this trial to me was having people sit in the courtroom, hearing all the things that I knew that the defense wanted to say about me. I feared that they would end up believing the lies about me and start to really question me as a person. I knew there was an element of morbid curiosity, but it made me feel even more insecure.

I also was feeling a great deal of mixed feelings toward our good friends since her husband worked at the public defenders' office with the women who were defending Johnathan. He was in an uncomfortable place, and I was uneasy being around him any longer because of the access he had to the information regarding the case. I didn't want to ask him what he was told or what he knew about the case, and I really didn't want to talk to him about the case at all. I will say, though, that he and his wife both sent me very encouraging and loving texts reminding me that God was with me. That meant so much to me! That was a priceless gift to me as it told me that they still remembered who I was and what my true nature and character were.

I had a lot of well-meaning friends who wanted to be there for me. Their motives were really born out of a desire to show support to me, and I appreciated that, but I still didn't want them in the courtroom, especially when I was up on the stand. I felt a need to protect them as much as a need to protect *me*. I had already been in the ring with Satan for round one via the defense attorney's "interview." I had tasted how vicious they could be.

Suzy did a wonderful job of communicating to the group of how this was distressing rather than helpful to me. She praised my support system, telling them how she had never seen anything quite like this before, and she was honored to be on the prosecution team in this case. That same sentiment was echoed by Brian and Erin, and although Rob didn't attend this incredible night, he had already communicated this same feeling.

That night before the trial was spirit filled. There was *no* denial who was in that room with us all as we sang and prayed. Erin, Suzy, and Brian all attended; and all were very touched by what they were seeing and witnessing. Suzy was incredibly choked up, and she was surprised at this and said she doesn't usually get so emotional when she talks to people. Prayers were said particularly for them as well, requesting that God would protect them and give them the right words at the right time in this battle. We all came away feeling peaceful even during the expectation of unpleasant things to come. This battle was about to become bloody, but the battle belonged to the Lord, and I knew that in my heart.

On the way to the courthouse that first day, I sat in the back of the car and cried and tried to keep it together. I was so nervous and uptight about what I knew was coming that I felt physically sick. I had a difficult time just trying to breathe. I was doing anything I could to find some peace in the storm. It was during these most grim times that I really honed in on my music. The song that was giving me the most strength and comfort during this time was the song "Eye of the Storm" by Ryan Stevenson.

I wish I could tell you an exact amount of times that this song would come on the radio and encourage me. Between certain scriptures that the Lord was giving to me to reassure me of his loving presence and protection and this song, I was literally saturated with his spirit.

The lyrics to this song are as follows:

> In the eye of the storm, you remain in control
>
> And in the middle of the war, you guard my soul
>
> You alone are the anchor, when my sails are torn
>
> Your love surrounds me in the eye of the storm

I would sing that part of the song and sob because my sails really were torn. I was in the middle of the biggest war of my life, and I had been attacked, not just physically but spiritually. God my Father really was my anchor in the storm, and I knew in my heart he remained in control.

> When the solid ground is falling out from underneath my feet
>
> Between the black skies, and my red eyes,
>
> I can barely see when I realize
>
> I've been sold out by my friends and my family
>
> I can feel the rain reminding me

This verse rang true because my skies were black, and my eyes were constantly red from crying. As I wrote earlier, I found out who really was my friend and who wasn't and who in my family would really stay by my side and who wouldn't. It was painful realization. The truth was that the only one I could truly count on to know the truth of all that had happened and still be there for me was the Lord. And the truth was that he loved me and was carrying me. My husband and kids were there for me, but they also had a lot to deal with as well.

> In the eye of the storm, you remain in control
>
> In the middle of the war, you guard my soul
>
> You alone are the anchor, when my sails are torn
>
> Your love surrounds me in the eye of the storm

This was a spiritual warfare. This wasn't just some random attack on me. I had reached into the dark and cold cave where Satan was holding someone hostage, and I dared to speak words of life and words of love and affirmation to his captive. I was a target, and Satan was mad.

> When my hopes and dreams are far from me,
>
> and I'm runnin' out of faith
>
> I see the future I picture slowly fade away
>
> And when the tears of pain and heartache are falling down my face
>
> I find my peace in Jesus's name

There are no words that can describe the depth of grief from what has happened to me. I worked for three and a half years to help this man. I had hoped and dreamed of his future and a restoration not only to himself but to his family and to the God who created him. I had to face the harsh reality that those dreams were now dead.

But I also had to find my peace and know that I really did do what I could, and I obeyed when I didn't want to when I first reached out to Johnathan.

> In the eye of the storm
>
> You remain in control (yes, you do, Lord)
>
> In the middle of the war, you guard my soul
>
> You alone are the anchor, when my sails are torn
>
> Your love surrounds me
>
> In the eye of the storm

After my first day on the stand, I was mentally and physically exhausted. But that was not the hardest part…yet. That was Suzy questioning me. I was on the stand for a total of six hours that day alone. She was so thorough because her plan was to take the sails out of the defense team and answer all the questions before they could ask them. She told me it would be much easier coming from her than from them. She was so right. That night, though, I saw how much God's love was surrounding me when I walked into my house. I was greeted with dozens of vases of brilliant-colored flowers in every corner of my house. Up the stairs, down the hallways, in the kitchen, in the dining room, in the living room, in the bathroom, in all the bedrooms, there were posters hung all over the house with Bible verses of encouragement and love and reassurance everywhere. My kitchen table was covered with cards and letters and scripture cards from many people who know and love us. I couldn't believe the outpouring of love. I was surrounded by his love and the prayers of those who had blessed us in this way.

When the test comes in and the doctor says I've only got a few months left It's like a bitter pill I'm swallowing; I can barely take a breath And when addiction steals my baby girl, and there's nothing I can do My only hope is to trust You I trust You, Lord

My only hope is to trust you. I trust you, Lord. Oh, how I prayed those words. I trust you Lord. He rewarded that trust and honored my faith.

> In the eye of the storm, you remain in control
>
> In the middle of the war, You guard my soul
>
> You alone are the anchor, when my sails are torn
>
> Your love surrounds me
>
> In the eye of the storm, you remain in control (yes, you do, Lord)
>
> In the middle of the war, you guard my soul
>
> You alone are the anchor, when my sails are torn
>
> Your love surrounds me in the eye of the storm,
>
> Oh, in the eye of, oh, in the eye of the storm

In the midst of this storm, Jesus guarded my soul. There were so many nasty things said to me during the trial from the defense attorney's. One that will never leave my mind was the question, "Was it flattering Barb, to have him push you up against the bushes and grind into you?" That question was straight from the lips of the devil. I looked at Suzy whose mouth fell open and to the jury who looked equally shocked and I took a deep breath before answering her question. My answer was calm and pointed and I was told full of dignity and poise. Inside I was screaming out nasty things I wanted to say in return, but when I took that breath I asked God to help me answer her nasty question.

> I know you're watching me
>
> When the storm is raging
>
> And my hope is gone

When my flesh is failing,

You're still holding on

When the storm is raging

And my hope is gone

When my flesh is failing

You're still holding on,

How many times I pleaded with the Lord to let the trial not happen. I prayed hard that Johnathan would just fess up to what he had done and spare me and my family of the whole ugly ordeal, but God said no. My grace is sufficient for you.

When the storm is raging (when the storm is raging)

And my hope is gone (and my hope is gone)

Even when my flesh is failing (flesh is failing)

You're still holding on, holding on

It isn't a simple cliché to say that the battle belongs to the Lord. It does. This was a spiritual battle, and God told me to rest in him and know he was going to bring about good for his glory and his purpose. He told me over and over, "Trust." When my life felt out of control and dark and hopeless, he gave me peace in the storm. I could not have emerged on the other side of this storm-tossed sea if it were not for his light shining on the waves to light the way.

The Lord is my Shepherd

I have all that I need

"My strength is made perfect in weakness."

He lets me rest in green meadows

He leads me beside peaceful streams

"My peace I give to you."

He renews my strength

The Lord is my strength and my song.

He guides me along right paths, bringing honor to his name

"Never will I leave you. Never will I forsake you."

Even when I walk through the darkest valley,

I will not be afraid, for you are close beside me

Can you see why this song was so encouraging to me? God was using the lyrics in this song to speak peace, courage, strength, love, confidence, and rest to my soul. He literally was enveloping me in each word, and I just love him for his constant presence and love to me and my family throughout this trial. As a matter of fact, I appreciated it so much I contacted Ryan Stevenson to tell him of my ordeal and how much his song helped me. Guess what? He responded. Now how cool is that! I love a real person behind the song on the radio. What a testament. It is truly such a blessing in the midst of the storm-tossed sea.

The seventh promise: "Whatever happens, conduct yourselves in a manner worthy of the gospel of Christ. Then, whether I come and see you or only hear about you in my absence, I will know that you stand firm in the one Spirit, striving together as one for the faith of the gospel without being frightened in any way by those who oppose you. This is a sign to them that they will be destroyed, but that you will be saved and that by God" (Philippians 1:27–28).

My twelve hours over a two-day period of time on the stand could have gone very badly if I had allowed myself to be overcome by the fear and dread that I had inside me. I hated to have to be in the room with Johnathan so close by. He made my skin crawl. I could see when I looked over at him that he was listening intently and most likely reliving things in his mind. It was insulting to see him sit there with a smug look on his face, but it was not lost on me that he never once looked up to peer at the jury or showed any kind of emotion. It got under my skin to see him smiling and laughing with his defense team before they had me on the stand. Even so, I kept my focus on the One who was really in control in that courtroom. I prayed constantly, thought of the inspiring words of songs and scriptures, and told my truth. And my truth has never changed, no matter how much others tried to twist it and flavor it to try and make Johnathan look innocent.

You see, no matter what your circumstances are, people are watching you. They want to know if when the rubber meets the road you will hold up to what you claim. I was cognizant that I was being watched and studied by many people in and out of my circle. They were curious if I would lose my faith or if my faith would bring me through. They wanted to know if my Jesus was *the* Jesus of the Bible, the one who saves, heals, and restores. They were watching me to see that it is okay to grieve and okay to be human and experience fear, pain, injustice, and disdain. They were watching me to see how a Christian can still love and shine in the midst of the storm. They were watching me to see if I was authentic or not. And guess what? They are still watching me.

God was telling me to not be frightened in any way. He was telling me that he was going to destroy my enemy and save me. My enemy isn't really Johnathan. My enemy is Satan. Johnathan was nothing but a tool he used to hurt and destroy me. Johnathan had a propensity already for allowing Satan to mess with him. He already had him in his clutches. I watched him fighting the battles over a period of over three years. I know this to be true. It comes back to what is in a man's heart overflowing into his life. He still had a choice in the matter, and he chose to listen to the wrong voice. Once again, my spirit was quieted with the calm reassurance of my loving Father, "The Lord will fight for you; you need only to be still" (Exodus 14:14).

THE FACE OF COURAGE

Forget about the battle.
You're here with me now.
Rest . . .

—God

It comes down to twelve people deciding whether or not I am lying or telling the truth. Twelve people who have to listen to all angles of each side. Twelve people who will size me up and size Johnathan up and decide based on information they were given.

Beyond a shadow of a doubt, they would decide that fate unanimously. My side was straight forward. I told my story and never changed it. Nearly twelve hours of questions and answers and accusations and innuendos. Did I make foolish decisions? Yes. Did I go down to the park on my own accord that day? Yes. Did I deserve what happened to me? No. Did I take part in it in any way? No.

The defense team did everything they could to try and make me look like a lovesick confused school girl. It was offensive on every level. I chose to not be in the courtroom for opening statements or any other part of the trial outside of my testimony and the closing arguments. I did this because I didn't want the jury to concentrate on watching me instead of hearing the testimony put before them.

Detective Bob Franke was on the stand for the better part of a day. They were terrible to him accusing him of poor police work. Why didn't they do this, and why didn't they do that? I felt horrible for him. He was a good officer, and he took me and my story very seriously. He was kind, compassionate, and thorough. Those who are trained professionals can tell when a person is just making up a wild story and when they are not. He believed me, and I was glad for it. I don't know what I would have done if I were treated like I was not telling the truth. That does happen to people who have been victim-ized, even to this day. To be grilled as he was and still come back with the determination that he had was incredible to see. Brian and Suzy came back very angry at the line of questioning and how much the defense tried to discredit Detective Franke. He was tired and frus-trated but happy to do his job, and when all was said and done, he did his best, and we all knew it.

I learned that my recorded interview with the lady officer that day at the CVA did not get recorded. I learned that while I was being questioned. The defense team seemed a little shocked that I was not privy to that information. They wanted to make a big deal out of it but couldn't. They were rude and mean to that officer as well, making her look like she was inept or intentionally tampering with evidence.

Over the six days of trial, I sat in the conference room a ball of emotions, holding my breath each time someone I knew or loved had to go and face the nasty questioning of the defense team. I was grate-ful beyond belief to have my brother-in-law and my sister-in-law were there with me as well as many friends and my counselor, Rob. They kept me sane. There were times when I would break down and cry and times when I just couldn't sit still. My phone was going off constantly from friends all over the US checking in on me and letting me know we were all in their prayers.

My friend Ann Marie took quite a beating on her day in court. They mocked her by accusing her of not being a good friend since she didn't know what had happened in detail. After all, if we were such good friends, why did she not know those details? They didn't want to give consideration to the fact I was totally a wreck and maybe I was too ashamed of what had happened to give my friends a detailed account of it. And then the question, how could she possibly not know I was suicidal? Why would I not tell her if we were so close? They mocked her for her faith in Jesus and made her feel horrible.

When they were done with her, she came back to the conference room, and as soon as she saw me, she burst into tears. I tried to calm her down and tell her that it was all a part of their nasty plan to undermine me and my character. I was so sorry that she was drug into it at all, but since she was with me that day after the rape, she knew better than anyone just how traumatized I really was. In the end, the truth was told, and that was all she could do.

Liz was a wonderful witness too. She was my "partner in crime," as I always jokingly said. We worked together so well. Liz knew me better than anyone else, outside of my family. We spent countless hours together talking about our "children" as we lovingly referred to the homeless here in Missoula. We are like two peas in a pod; both of us have a heart for service and a ton of love to give. We are both compassionate and patient seeing the best in people where the rest of the world looks past them.

Yes, we saw the hurt and the dirt and the grime, and have no doubt, we smelled it too! But we also looked inside the outer shell and could connect with the being *inside*. The ones who just wanted to be loved and validated. We saw the best and the worst in these people. We held their hands, hugged their necks, prayed with them, talked with them, listened to them, counseled them, and on more than one occasion provided for them. Our provision could be a coat, a sweater, a blanket, a pair of shoes, clean pants for those who had soiled theirs, hygiene products, laundry, and showers. Sometimes, it would be medical care they needed. I bandaged more than one person and cleaned more nasty face wounds than I can count.

More than once, we had people with seizures from lack of medication and/or drugs and alcohol abuse, or a mental breakdown requiring hospitalization. Many times, we held people as they cried from the hurts they were carrying inside from family members. Some were gay and cut off from their families. Some were former convicts. Most had issues with alcohol. Some were driven to that lifestyle because of drug habits they couldn't kick. Some were just teens who were lost and looking for direction. Some were lazy and had no desire to change. Some were volatile and scary. Some were just crazy. But the common thing they all had was the knowledge that Liz and I truly loved them. And because of that love, we truly mourned when they would die from drug or alcohol abuse or suicide.

And it didn't stop at the doors of the mission. We would see these same people on the streets and always make sure to talk to them and encourage them. We were the ones the homeless trusted and would come to when they needed help or just an ear. Believe it or not, I was only asked for money once in the five years I had worked with the mission. We were loved and respected. More than once I would get serenaded by a man each time I came to serve, and he would sing my name out and make a silly song. When Liz and I came through those doors, a lighthearted atmosphere would ensue. It was a blessing, and we loved what we did.

Liz was awesome in the courtroom. She was able to talk to the jury and look directly at them as she explained me to them. She also was able to explain to them why I felt compelled to help Johnathan and reach out to him as I did time and time again. She knew from our many conversations that I felt very trapped. I knew he needed me, and I also knew he needed other people to help him. I just couldn't walk away and leave him without someone who truly cared about his well-being. That alone was my biggest failure.

Still, sitting and waiting was pure torture to me. I worried and prayed each time a friend of mine was on the stand. I would wait while holding my breath to see how they were doing and how the trial was going. A large part of me wanted to be in there to hear it all, but a larger part of me wrapped myself in a cocoon of protection and waited for the end result, knowing God was in control.

After each small recess, the county attorneys would come in and update us on how things were going. Suzy and Brian and my advocate Erin were always very upbeat about the direction the trial was going. They were feeling considerably confident despite the nastiness of the public defenders and their ploys. Still, we all knew that no matter what, it was twelve people who would ultimately decide one way or the other how this was going to end.

I had two other friends who were put on the stand too. Crystal and Peggy, thankfully, were only up for a fleeting time in comparison to Liz and Ann Marie. All of us were instructed we couldn't talk to each other prior to testimony at the trial. It was an incredible burden to us all as I needed my friends, and they were aware of this fact and wanted to be there for me as much as they could. When Crystal and Peggy took the stand, they repeated what had already been said by Liz and Ann Marie about me and my state of being before and after the rape and how different I was now. Each one was underlining the same story, giving more credence to the state's case against Johnathan with each word spoken.

After all of my friends were done on the stand, we had a mini reunion in the conference room with many hugs and tears and prayers. The worst part of the storm was now over for most of us. But there were still more witnesses. One was an expert on trauma who had never met me before and didn't even know my name or the details of the case. Two witnesses who were called by the defense knew me really well. One was the case worker who had originally worked with Johnathan and me at the WMMHC, and the other was the director of the mission. As it turned out, neither of these witnesses were called. We can only surmise that their testimony would have helped the prosecution's case more than the defense. This is based off the interviews conducted in pretrial. Both spoke highly of me, and the work I had done with and for Johnathan. The last to be put through the fire was my husband, Al.

It was now Thursday, day five of the trial. We were all starting to wonder if this would be over this week or recess into the next week. The trial was already taking twice as long as predicted, and the jury was getting weary. That morning getting ready for the coming testimony of my husband we were a bundle of nerves. He was literally sick with anticipation but was also filled with a strong resolve to make sure he was heard. On the way to the courthouse, he and I were alone in the car. I reached over and grabbed his hand and started to pray peace over my husband and strength to not get baited and lose his temper.

Al is not a violent man. He is strong, steady, kind, and firm. He is also witty, charming, and well loved by tons of people. As a couple, we are well-known and respected. As a family, we were known as a tight-knit family who truly love each other and enjoy spending time together. So when the defense's tactic was to try and paint him as a controlling and overbearing husband, it was almost more than he could take. His wit is instant, and he is very quick on the draw when he's being attacked. But in this situation, he had to be very careful to use restraint and not go there as it could be detrimental to the case. If he had tried, he probably could've made them look like monkeys with their questions. This would have been perfectly justified if he had chosen to go that route.

Al was in the courtroom for nearly five hours in total. It was a mentally exhausting ordeal for all of us. I was pacing the room and hallway, and each time I looked at the clock, it had barely moved from the last time. The tension I felt in my body was skyrocketing. My hands were shaking, and my head was pounding. I was sick to my stomach and had severe intestinal issues. I kept trying to tell myself that God was in control and he was going to work all this out for his glory. But going through all that mental stress and anguish is superhard, and letting the Lord work it all out while we waited was an excruciating process. Still, I kept my trust in him, knowing that no matter how the jury decided, I had told the truth, and I knew God knew that.

Rob took me into another room and helped me with some guided meditation to try and center me and help me calm down. I broke down in that room and sobbed freely, letting some of the tension and stress out of my body. I was worried to death that Al was being portrayed as this awful person when in fact he was so far from that! I hated Johnathan even more for what he was putting us through, and I hated his sleazy defense attorneys just as much. I seethed with anger at all of it. But, in all of it, I never turned my back on God.

I knew he understood my emotions and was patient with me as I worked through them. Finally, Al was back with us. He was ashen and very upset, but strong. I was proud to hear that he was able to control his words and speak to the accusations about me and himself and us as a couple. God had been with my husband covering him with his grace and his spirit of wisdom. Suzy and Brian came back and said he was a rock star and were very full of praise for how well he held it together.

We had a debriefing session with Suzy and Brian before they returned to the courtroom for more theater. The news was that the trial would wrap up this day, and the next day would be for closing arguments and finally letting the jury go to deliberate. It was finally coming to an end, and we all breathed a collective sigh of relief with this news.

Things were gearing up, and we were all wondering how the closing arguments would go. I understood Suzy would start the closing arguments, and then the defense would give their closing arguments, but then the prosecution would have the last word. This was so reassuring to us all. Then as we were getting ready to end the day, a bombshell hit Suzy. She had a family emergency and had to leave. We knew that Brian was going to be the one who did the closing arguments instead of Suzy. Although we were sad for Suzy, we felt that Brian was more than capable of handling the closing arguments, and we knew it would be just fine. We all hugged Suzy and assured her that we understood and sent her out to take care of her family emergency. I felt bad for her on two fronts... one, because of her emergency, but, two, because I knew how much she enjoyed doing closing arguments and how much she was looking forward to saying all she had prepared.

One would think on the eve of such an incredibly huge day I would not sleep. Truth be told, I was so completely exhausted that I actually *did* sleep that night. I woke in the morning with a sense of peace going into the day. This was a gift from the Lord. My sweet little family and I held onto each other in the early morning as we prepared to go into town and listen to the last efforts of the prosecution and defense teams as they would try to persuade the jury in the last round. We had done all that we could do. The rest was up to the Lord and the jury.

Al and I and our kids found a spot in the front row to the right of the jury box. It wasn't so they could peer at us, but because we didn't want to miss any of the things that were said and because we also wanted to see Johnathan's reaction to all of it. I, for one, wanted to watch him to see if there was any glimmer of sadness or remorse for his actions. Disclaimer... there wasn't. Several friends were there with us along with our family members. Because the trial had gone so long, one brother had to go back home before this point, and my niece had to return home as well. Both were there in spirit, though.

Johnathan, on the other hand, had nobody there to support him. Not a single family member to be seen. Despite all he had done to me and our family, I found this to be extremely sad as it only underlined the truth of my point about Johnathan, pushing everyone away who ever tried to care for him, especially his family. I had a suspicion that his family was not there because they were not told about the timing of the trial. I had an inkling that he had stated he didn't want them to be there.

Things started very punctually, and the courtroom was full. Brian was amazing. He was calm, pointed, and firm in his statements to the jury. He pointed out many things about Johnathan that I was not aware of prior to this case. The courtroom was very quiet apart from Brian as he outlined the facts of the case. The jury listened intently, and we all waited with hearts thumping out of control in our chests. After a while, Brian finished his speech, and we had a short ten-minute recess.

Next up was Johnathan's public defender. She proceeded to throw darts at what Brian had said and especially tried to concentrate on my response that day. She said, "Oh, I have no doubt that some people freeze when they are faced with a traumatic situation.

But Barb Jenkins did not freeze," while pointing her finger at me. In her estimation, I could have simply just put my hands up and shoved him away. I was seething with anger underneath. She tried her best to say that I had wanted to have sex with him, and he rebuffed me, so, therefore, I was upset and embarrassed. You can imagine how that makes me feel, even now. My husband was telling me to be still and be quiet while we sat there as I was getting very incensed. He was afraid I would be asked to leave if I couldn't contain it. I was doing a lot of deep breathing to try and calm myself down. I was visibly shaking and frustrated.

While the defense attorney was talking, the jury members were looking over at my kids and studying them. They were obviously compassionate toward them knowing how hard it must be for them to hear someone talking about their mom in the manner that I was being talked about. Both were either in tears or close to tears. I was in tears too, and I felt completely helpless at that point.

After she finished her statement, Brian took the stand again and shot holes soundly through all the things the defense had said. He reminded the jury of the facts of the case and underlined all the testimony about me and my character versus that of Johnathan's. He reminded them that they needed to stay within the guidelines of the jury instructions and what would and wouldn't be an acceptable outcome.

At long last, it was over. All the testimony was finished. The battles had been fought, and the blood had been spilled. The knives that were sharpened were used on me, and the armor I had worn had served me well. My spirit had been through the worst war in my existence, and I was still here to say I survived. The judge delivered last instructions to the jury and sent them out around twelve thirty for lunch and deliberations.

Knowing that the jury could be out for a long time or a brief time, we ordered pizza and had it delivered. The hours started ticking away, and I was full of nervous energy I reminded myself that the jury was tired and needed refreshed, so it would take about a half an hour to eat lunch. One o'clock. I remember thinking, "Now they are for sure in chambers talking about the case." I wondered who the foreman of the jury would be. I wondered if they had heard enough to know that what I said happened really did happen the way I said it did. I wondered if his demeanor in the trial was making an impression on them. I wondered if the faces of my children were weighing on their hearts. I wondered how long it would be. I feared with it being Friday that the jury might need to go into the following week. I wondered if my time on the stand had made a good impression on them.

Two o'clock. My fears were getting the best of me. What if they found him not guilty? What if they decided to say he was guilty of a misdemeanor instead of a felony? What if they believed the lies about me? What if? If he were to be found not guilty, how long would it be before he attacked me again? Would he also come after my family? And the old familiar self-doubt and self-blame started to poke its ugly head in at me again. I had worked long and hard to come to a place of healing where I realized that this was not a true statement.

Going on three o'clock. I had to get out of this room. I had to go pray. I asked Peggy to come with me and find a place where we could be alone and pray together. I took my cell phone along with me, but I didn't tell everyone where we were going. Peggy and I found a room down the hall that was not being used and stepped into it. We sat down in the chair and talked for a bit. Then we held each other's hands and entered the throne room of God. We offered our praise to God for his presence throughout the trial and the entire process. We praised him for showing his mightiness to all who were involved. We asked him to guide the jury to make a swift decision and that the decision would be a conviction. While we were praying, my phone was ringing incessantly. I didn't want to disturb Peggy in the middle of her prayer, so I waited until we said amen before looking at my phone. I had missed several calls from several people and had several text messages. The jury had reached a decision!

I literally flew down the hallway of the county attorney's office and ran to the courtroom. I had thankfully not missed anything, and the jury had not been ushered into the courtroom yet. I was more nervous than ever waiting for this decision to be announced. I knew from talk that when a jury comes back quickly it is usually a guilty verdict, but I was cautioned that it can also mean the other outcome was true.

The jury was ushered into the courtroom, and court was back in session. The judge asked the jury if they had reached a decision. The jury said they had and handed the verdict to the court reporter. The judge opened the decision and briefly glanced in my direction and handed it back to the court reporter. The judge asked the jury to state their decision. Guilty as charged. Each one had to state their name and confirm that their decision was guilty. This was an incredible and insurmountable moment suspended in time. Guilty. Guilty. Guilty. Guilty. Guilty. Guilty. Guilty. Guilty. Guilty. Guilty. Guilty. Guilty. Twelve jurors, one decision. One major victory in finding justice and righting a terrible wrong. Twelve souls who saw the truth and decreed to the court that I was in fact telling the truth. I cried grateful tears and looked desperately toward the jury to catch an eye and say thank you to them.

The jury was officially dismissed, and they began filing out of the courtroom. Johnathan hollered out to them, "Why are you doing this to me? I didn't do anything! I didn't do anything to her!" Then he clenched his fists and twisted his face in an evil glare and stood there in a threatening pose toward me. We walked out of the courtroom, and the bailiff proceeded to remove Johnathan from the courtroom to be returned to the county detention center to await sentencing. I prayed that his outburst and body language were not lost on the judge.

The eighth promise: "But I delight in my weaknesses, in insults, in hardships, in persecutions, in difficulties. For when I am weak, then I am strong" (2 Corinthians 12:9–10). The one constant in this tumultuous time of my life was the fact that God was telling me he was with me and supplying me with the strength and courage I needed. One of the most encouraging things I had heard along the way was that if you were going through major persecution or hardship to count yourself blessed as God has seen you as worthy to suffer for his name. Another way to look at it was that I was a big enough threat to Satan that he thought he needed to shut me down.

In Job, Satan was roaming about the earth then came and stood before the Lord. He asked him, "Where did *you* come from?" Satan answered him, "From roaming the earth and going back and forth in it." Then God offered him Job. "Have you considered my servant Job?" And if you have read the Bible, then you already know the devastation that came upon Job after that conversation. Was God mad at him? No. Did he not love him anymore? Of course he did! Didn't he know what all Satan would do to Job? Yes. Did he allow it? Yes. God knew Job was a "blameless and upright man … no one on earth like him." He knew that in the end Job's ordeal would be used as a tool for good to show God's glory and goodness.

My situation is not remotely like Job's was, to be sure. However, my devastation was just as real. The fallout was painful, I felt isolated and unloved, and I too had "friends" say terrible things to me. I too had others wondering why I didn't just blame God. I too knew that God was going to use me and this situation as a tool for good to show his glory and goodness.

Fast-forward to the New Testament, and we see multiple examples of suffering unduly. Stephen was stoned to death. Paul was imprisoned, stoned, flogged, beaten, shipwrecked, and relentlessly persecuted. Peter and Johnathan were arrested and flogged. Jesus himself was crucified after suffering greatly! Luke 12:4 says not to fear those who can kill the body, but rather to fear the one who can kill the soul. I know from hearing the word of God repeatedly that no matter what man does to me, I am secure in my salvation. I can't imagine my life lived without that knowledge. It is the sweetest of assurances in my arsenal. Every one of the disciples, with exception to Judas who betrayed Jesus and committed suicide, was tortured and put to death. Their deaths varied by being burned alive, stoned, boiled in hot oil, speared to death, clubbed and beaten to death, and crucified, as our Lord was (Peter upside down). But to be counted "worthy" to suffer for his sake is a compliment to the Christian. I didn't say it is easy, only that it is a compliment.

My ordeal is far from a compliment or an honor in the human sense. But in the eternal sense, to be such a threat to Satan that he would try to destroy me in this way and yet have God fight for me so completely—now *that* is an honor. That he would love me that much to even care what I in my insignificance was going through and stay with me by my side—now that is humbling. I truly can't describe adequately what that kind of love feels like, and I know in my imperfection against the holiness of Christ, I can never even begin to repay him with the absolute and unhindered praise and adoration he deserves. But I do know this ... I can always try. Until I take my last breath, I will keep on trying.

BURYING JANE DOE

After the trial was completed, I found myself in a different place. I wasn't completely okay, but I wasn't out of my mind with worry anymore about all the "what-if" scenarios that kept plaguing my mind. I literally felt as though I had gone into the ring with Satan, stared him right in the eyes, and fought the bloodiest battle I have ever endured. But that's the thing. I endured. And because I had endured, God won!

I remember having a conversation with Suzy before the trial. I told her that no matter how the complete process ended up, I knew she did her best, and I knew that I had told the truth. That is something nobody could take from me. No matter how much Johnathan wanted to twist the events of that day or any other for that matter, going through this process was worth it no matter come what may. Why? Because I stood up to him and called him out for what he did. And if I can stop him from hurting another woman like this, it is more than worth it!

My central nervous system was shot. It took me about a full three weeks after the trial was over for my body to *start* to simmer down to some form of normal, even though "normal" for me was still not good and hadn't been since October 12, 2015. Everything I ate caused me to have an upset stomach, and I had so much tension in my body that my migraines were off the charts out of control.

Peggy pulled me aside one day prior to the trial and talked to me excitedly about a grief retreat that was coming to Stevensville, Montana, at the Burnt Fork Ranch. It was called Spark of Life and was free with a deposit of five hundred dollars. I misunderstood the deposit and thought that, because of all the work we had missed, there was no way we had an extra five hundred dollars sitting around, and so I didn't follow up. On the day that Peggy was testifying, she asked me if we had registered or not. I told her no because of the deposit. She was mortified as she explained to me that the deposit would not be cashed *and* would be returned after the retreat, as long as we showed up. She knew the retreat only had so many spots and thought it had filled up by now. I promised her I would go online and check it out that night, which I did.

Spark of Life was full for Stevensville, but I went ahead and contacted them anyway. I talked to the coordinator, and she said to go ahead and register even though it was full as who knew except God, that an opening could come up. I registered us and sent the deposit in just in case someone else cancelled. I told Peggy, "If God wants us there, he will work it out." As it turned out, I got an e-mail three days later... we had secured our place at the retreat since it is first come first serve, and we got our deposit in before one of the other participants. I wasn't sure exactly what we were in for, but I knew from Peggy that it was something she fully believed would help us in our healing process.

October 6–9, 2016, was the date of the retreat. How timely was that! Only three days later would be the one-year anniversary of my greatest loss. Our greatest loss. The loss of so much that words can't even remotely describe it. It was monumental, and I dreaded that day and didn't know what to do to prepare myself. I knew it was weighing on my husband's and kids' minds and hearts as well. What would any of us do with the remnants of life before Johnathan raped me? Where were the pieces that we still needed, those elusive pieces to this giant puzzle, to put us and our family back together again?

Spark of Life was our springboard for our "new normal." Think of fish in a tank. When a fish is taken from water, it no longer can "breathe." It flips and flops around and tries with all its might to escape the suffocating air and get back into the water where it is able to live. However, if the water is bad, it still will not be healthy. Without the water, it cannot live. We are much like a fish when it is taken from it's safe environment, the one in which it lives and thrives and survives in. When the tank becomes contaminated, the owner takes the fish and removes them from the contamination and places it into another body of water while the tank is cleaned. If the tank isn't cleaned, eventually the fish will die.

Not that we are fish, but when our lives become so polluted with grief and sadness and heartache, we just simply need to let the keeper of our world (God) remove us from our contaminated surroundings while he cleans it out for us. For Al and me, that removal was a picturesque retreat in the Bitterroot Valley in Montana for three solid days of pampering and soul-searching with others who were grieving in their own unique ways too.

While driving down the dirt road to the beautiful ranch where the retreat was being held, the weather was something else! Dark clouds abounded all around us, and the rain was heavy. But then off in the distance of the mountains was the most humongous rainbow, and it was *so* bright! The sun was shining over there. I was so amazed and mesmerized by this rainbow I insisted Al pull over so we could try to capture it on our cameras. It was like God was saying to us personally, "See? I have placed a sign in the heavens for *you* to tell you that you are going to be okay."

When we arrived at the ranch, we were greeted in the driveway by our hosts, and they immediately hugged us. These strangers to us were looking at us as though we were long-lost family returning from a long journey. And, indeed, this had been a long, long journey, and we were sorely tired. We were instructed to follow them in our car to our own cabin. It was about a five-minute drive. The "cabin" was a marvelous miniresort.

We were instructed that we didn't need to bother with bedding, pillows, towels, shampoo, conditioner, soap, or anything that we would need as they would provide for us. We only needed to bring ourselves and some extra clothes and our battered hearts.

Inside the cabin was fully stocked with everything we needed in the kitchen as well as in the bathroom. Even the fridge was stocked with food, water, pop, and whatever we would want for a snack. The kitchen table had a welcome note on it and a basket of fruit and a bowl of chocolates! The decor was rustic yet homey. There was a gas fireplace, leather furniture, soft lights, throw blankets, wall mounts of various wildlife, and a huge bed that required stairs to get into; and it just felt like a home away from home. The bathroom was large and had a big walk in shower and a nice claw-foot tub with an assortment of bath salts if we wanted to soak. There was even a hair dryer and curling iron, toothpaste and toothbrushes, combs, and various supplies for us both. It was an incredibly beautifully rustic hideaway, and perfect for a respite. The sign over the door read, "Come away to a place of rest" (Mark 6:31). As a matter of fact, our neighbors cabin was the spot where the author of *The Shack* wrote part of the book! It was a beautiful slice of heaven, and it was all for us.

We deposited our belongings at our cabin and headed back to the lodge where everyone was preparing for dinner. The lodge was also beautiful and rustic and had an unmistakable feeling of home sweet home, only in this case, much, much nicer than our abode! We made small talk with our dinner mates and acquainted ourselves with each other. After dinner, we retired to the main living room and sat in a circle.

That first night was a hard one. We were instructed to go around the circle and introduce ourselves and tell what or who we were grieving. Some of the stories were absolutely heart-wrenching—stories of murdered loved ones, drug overdoses, cancer battles lost, suicides, and deaths in every age group. Some of the participants were literally only a couple of weeks out from losing their loved ones, and their pain was very raw. Some had lost spouses; some had lost children. I cried as each story unfolded as my heart felt their own grief. When it came to me, I said my story was a little different as the person I had lost was me. I shared briefly how we had just been through hell and back and how much I had struggled just to breathe another breath each second of each day.

That night was sobering for sure. But it was good to get it all out there. No secrets, no judgment, just compassion and love. Our hosts promised us they would not try to "fix" us. There would be no crosstalk, no apologies for emotions, no stopping each other's emotions, no advice unless asked for. Just pure raw honesty. Although our hosts clearly were Christians, this was not even about proselytizing people. The focus was on healing and moving forward, nothing more, nothing less. How refreshing! We were safe here.

Throughout the weekend, we were paired with a group of three to four people, not the person we came with. So Al was paired with two other men, and I was paired with two other women. These beautiful souls were such a blessing to me, and I grew very close to them throughout the next couple of days. We had opportunity to write our thoughts on certain subjects and then read them to our team without interruption. We then could ask the person who read what they wrote if they were done speaking and if they would like a hug. But *no* advice, just listening and showing empathy.

The *Grief Recovery Handbook, 20th Anniversary Expanded Edition* by John W. James and Russell Friedman, Collins Living 2009, says, "Grief is about a broken heart, not a broken brain." It reminds me again of that conversation with my friend who was so shocked when she realized I was grieving after Johnathan raped me. My heart was broken. My brain was on overload for sure, but the underlying issue was my heart had been damaged and broken. I needed healing, not judgment from those who just couldn't understand my pain or the depth of it.

One of the greatest myths I have had to battle was the thought process others carry that says, "It's been a year, so you should be over this by now." One of the lessons of the weekend was to underscore the fact that grief is different for all of us, and each of us has our own timeline to healing. Time does not heal all wounds. It does help us to live around the wounds, though.

When my son was little, I was frustrated that he was saying hurtful things to me or behaving in an undesirable fashion at times. Don't get me wrong. He was a wonderful child, but I wanted to make an impression on him that words and actions can make lasting impressions on others

I took a piece of wood and got some colored thumbtacks. Each time he did something that was not nice or said something that was not nice, I would put a thumbtack in the board. He started to notice this, and I told him those were holes he was making in my heart. So then when he would do something thoughtful or kind, I would remove a thumbtack. Soon he had very few thumbtacks. But the holes were still there.

Eventually, I started to patch the holes with filler. I talked to him about how the board didn't use to have holes in them, and even though we could fill the holes, it would look different and feel different. I told him that our hearts are much like this board. When someone does or say something hurtful to us, our hearts get a hole in them. And when that person says they are sorry, that hole gets patched, but the heart is no longer the same as it was before the hole was put there.

I think this simple lesson I taught my son can be applied to any situation in our lives that hurt us. Our hearts get hit and pitted by the storms of life. In my case, I lived through horrors of abuse as a child, and more than once was I raped as an adult. In my case, apologies never came, except from my dad, who was physically and verbally abusive when I was little. My heart was tattered and torn, but it was patched up and made as good as new by the Maker of my heart. Although he had healed me of the painful realities of my past and allowed my heart to trust again, time did not fully heal the wound. I found this truth to be especially true after Johnathan raped me as it threw me back forty years to an eight-year-old child's instinct and native defense mechanisms. All the work I had done along the way to be whole came crashing down around me. It was all there again. So, no, time does not heal all wounds. It just makes it easier to live around.

One of the things we were required to do was make a Loss Story for our entire life. That was a chore. I had to go way back to my earliest memories and list things on my timeline. I also needed to list the emotions that went along with each event on the timeline. Each loss could be viewed as a positive or negative loss. For example, when my mom and dad divorced, Dad was out of the house. He was my dad, so that was a loss. But it was a positive loss as it meant that the abuse was over. Marriage can be a positive or negative loss: positive, as you lose your individual status and become a couple or a team; negative, because you now have another person to consider in all you say and do. It is the same with parenting. Having kids is a wonderful gift. It can also be a boatload of stress as it requires a lifetime commitment to take care of those gifts. It was a very neat exercise in which I realized there were some big points along the way that shaped me into the person I am now. It was also very cathartic to list the emotions that went along with those events.

Al and I were not allowed to discuss with each other the things that we wrote about or shared in our groups. It was complete confidentiality for each participant, and that included our spouses. We discussed some things in general vague terms but only relating to our own personal story and not the stories of our group partners.

Perhaps one of the most challenging parts for me with the retreat was my Relationship Story with Johnathan. Much like the Loss Story, the Relationship Story was a timeline of events in our time in each other's lives, along with the emotions that went with it. It was hard to write anything positive or kind about Johnathan in my timeline as I was still so full of pain and anger at him. I hated that I had ever believed that this man could ever be anything but an evil person who had violated me in the most ruthless way. Talking to my group about this was extremely hard. Thankfully, they just let me cry and then hugged me until I pulled away.

The blessings to me after recording this timeline were crystal clear. God's blessings to me throughout the whole ordeal from

October 12, 2015, to that moment and for that matter since then were abundant. There was no way I could not be grateful to him. Again, I was reminded of the constant flow of communication coming to me from the Lord. "I am with you. I am fighting for you. I love you. You are mine. This is *my* battle. Rest. Trust." Although I know I didn't deserve what happened to me, I still have regrets that I didn't pay more attention to my warnings. Even so, God has lovingly been restoring me and showing me my worth and value in His eyes.

Another exercise we did was to write a letter saying good-bye. In it, we were to include regrets such as any apologies owed, resentments, remembrances, and conclude it with good-bye. In our case, an apology was not applicable. This was something that Johnathan did to me, not the other way around. I still have no idea to this day what Al's letter said, and as far as I know, he doesn't know what mine said. However, I have decided to share my letter of good-bye in hopes it can help bring a healing path to another.

> Dear Johnathan,
>
> I have been thinking of our relationship and I have a few things to say to you. First of all, I don't feel I have anything to apologize to you for, so I won't.
>
> I reached out to you four years ago as an act of faith and obedience to my Lord, Jesus Christ. It was not a comfortable thing for me, especially at first. I went way outside my comfort zone to reach you because I really believed God wanted me to. Why? Because He loved you so much and you needed someone to tell you so. And I did. Many times. God put me at the mission and he brought you through those doors. None of what transpired is a surprise to God.
>
> When I reached out to you on a consistent basis, you began a miraculous transformation. All of us were just amazed at God and the work He was doing with you. Your family was able to have hope, and especially your mom. When she died so unexpectedly, I was happy to be there for you as your friend.

But then you betrayed me and my trust. You trapped me and assaulted me. I chose to forgive you and give you the benefit of the doubt because I knew you were confused and grieving your mom. I made excuses for your horrible behavior.

I stayed the course with you. I made sure you got into housing after thirteen years of living on the streets. You had food, money, clothes, health and mental care and a roof over your head. You had every tool for success at your disposal because I did God's will and helped you. Then you did it again, this time scarier and more violent. You may recall I was so pissed at you; incredibly angry! And I confronted you. You cried and apologized and said you'd never do it again. I forgave you. Again. But I pulled away significantly and prayed earnestly for you.

I worried that if I walked away that you'd have nobody. I know now that it may have been true, but that wasn't ever my burden to carry. You saw me in July and attempted to put me in your closet. That is when I finally said, "No more." You wouldn't have that chance to hurt me or scare me again. Then you harassed me by text and phone until I put the restraining order on you. Once again, you apologized. I didn't accept your apology. You were told to stay away from me. You did for a while, then you didn't.

Johnathan, I am angry at you. You've filled me with rage and hurt so deep I can barely breathe. But I forgive you. Not because you deserve it, but because I don't want you to have that kind of control over me, and because I love Jesus Christ and I belong to Him. He wants me to. This is a daily decision.

I still to this day hold to the truth that the things I shared with you were what God wanted me to say. You were made for a reason. Your life had and still has a purpose. I pray for your soul because where you're at is an awful place to be and God's heart aches for you to see Him and His love and grace.

I forgive you Johnathan. But I never want you around me, my family or life again. I hope you will admit to yourself and to God the sins you've committed against me and repent so you can be saved. After all, that is why Jesus even came to the earth in the first place.

May you find peace, forgiveness and grace in the arms of Jesus, and find your restoration in Him.

Good-bye, Johnathan.

Barbie

It isn't important to me for him to read those words or to even hear them from me. What is important is that I was able to find an avenue that was healthy to express myself and really begin to lay Jane Doe to rest.

On the last day of the retreat, we had a very special time of fellowship with prayer and the Lord's supper. It was completely voluntary for any who wanted to come, and thankfully everyone attended. We prayed for each and every person and the burdens on their hearts. It was a time of release and renewal. After this, we had breakfast, then proceeded to the last part of the retreat.

We were each given a note card to write on. We were to write something on it and then tie it to a balloon to be released as a group. My note card said, "Hello, my name is Jane Doe. I was raped a year ago. If you find this card, please do an act of kindness for someone in my honor and in the honor of all who are victimized in this way. Look up and know that you are loved." I tied my note to the balloon, and with a heart bursting with a waterfall of tears ready to spill, I went outside and waited for all the others to join me on the lawn. We listened to specially chosen music, and on the countdown, we all let our balloons go. I watched mine disappear into the heavens, and along with my flowing tears, I felt a load of pain released from my heart.

I know it was only symbolic, and some may think it was cheesy, but in fact, it was very powerful healing. I promised myself that I would do something for me and my family in the next month to show them that I was truly healing. I wasn't sure yet what that would be, but I was determined to figure it out.

We left the retreat in higher spirits than we had been in a year. We could communicate better without being hesitant of being too triggering and the closeness we had only deepened. The loads we had been carrying had been lifted significantly by those who were sharing in our grief without judgment and without offering advice. Our drive home was bittersweet. We didn't really want to leave our respite, but we missed our kids and were anxious to see them again. God had poured his love and his spirit over us, and we were blessed indeed.

At home, I pondered over what I wanted to do. Then it came to me. Much like the balloon release, I now knew what I needed to do. It would be extremely hard, but I knew it needed to be done. I called my advocate Erin and asked her if she would go with me on the twelfth. I wanted to go back to the scene of the crime and face it. I also wanted to put Jane to rest in the same spot that she was conceived. Thankfully, Erin was more than happy to go with me.

That morning of October 12, 2016, I was filled with fear. I hated going anywhere near McCormick Park since Johnathan had raped me. So to intentionally go there and go back to that very spot filled me with a sense of fear, anxiety, and apprehension. Even though I had all those feelings, I had an even stronger resolve to do what I came to do. I brought along a couple of paint pens and a marker.

Erin and I walked down to the riverbank where I had been attacked. I described to her the events of that day a year ago and how much fear I had felt. I searched for a rock that I could use as a headstone, and I found one. It was rectangular and large enough to write on but not too large I couldn't toss it. I picked the one up that I chose, and it was covered with dirt on one side. I turned the rock on end and banged it against another rock to loosen the dirt, and the rock split perfectly into two identical slabs! How perfect! Now I had a lighter rock, but could still write on it and then throw it into the river.

I wasn't sure how the paint pen would work on the rock, but as it turned out, it worked like a charm. I wrote, "Good-bye, Jane Doe. RIP 10/12/15–10/12/16," and I threw the rock as hard as I could and buried Jane Doe in the water by the bridge. Erin took my phone and captured it in pictures for me. The look of determination on my face says it all. And when I threw that rock in the water, I took back me, Barb Jenkins. I no longer needed the security and anonymity of Jane Doe. I made a statement to Johnathan, although he wasn't there to see it, that I was stronger. I was a survivor and no longer his victim. I felt victorious and euphoric! I couldn't wait to tell my family!

The ninth promise: "This is what the Lord, the God of your father David, says: I have heard your prayer and seen your tears; I will heal you" (2 Kings 20:5).

When I read those words, I am reminded of the tenderness of the Lord to me. His gentle ways and compassion to me have been my healing balm. He has restored me, and he continues to bind up my wounds.

May she rest in peace.

THE NEW YOU

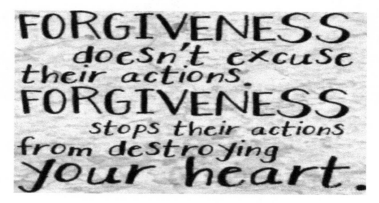

Forgiveness doesn't excuse their actions.

Forgiveness stops their actions from destroying your heart.

So how do you feel? Are you happy about the outcome? These were the questions I most heard after the sentencing hearing was over. Before I go into the answers to these questions, maybe I should start by talking about this big day in our lives. Sentencing day.

The last month leading up to this tremendous day was filled with a ton of emotions. First, Johnathan had been sent to Warm Springs State Mental Hospital to be evaluated. The judge suggested it to make sure the defense would not try to hold up sentencing any more than they already had. So he was sent there at the end of November 2016. He was not brought back until February 23, 2017, nearly ninety days later.

That very day, Al and I sat in Suzy's office with Brian and Erin and read the reports submitted by the different people who had done evaluations on him. One was the psychosexual evaluation where he would be listed as either a Tier 1, 2, or 3 offender. It determined his likelihood of reoffending and how violent he was. One report was done by a psychologist hired by the defense to determine the degree of mental illness and also to determine if he was a candidate for mental disease or defect in sentencing. The other was another evaluation done by another psychologist on staff at the state hospital.

All three reports agreed that he has mental issues, but they also agreed that he *was* able to understand the law and be able to conform to it, so, therefore, did not qualify for the mental disease or defect in sentencing as prescribed by Montana State Law. There was a difference in opinion regarding his diagnosis. One said he had a schizotypal personality disorder. Wikipedia describes it this way:

> A disorder characterized by eccentric behavior and anomalies of thinking and affect which resemble those seen in schizophrenia, though no definite and characteristic schizophrenic anomalies have occurred at any stage. There is no dominant or typical disturbance, but any of the following may be present:
>
> - Inappropriate or constricted affect (the individual appears cold and aloof);
>
> - Behavior or appearance that is odd, eccentric or peculiar;
>
> - Poor rapport with others and a tendency to withdraw socially;
>
> - Odd beliefs or magical thinking, influencing behavior and inconsistent with subcultural norms;
>
> - Suspiciousness or paranoid ideas;
>
> - Obsessive ruminations without inner resistance, often with dysmorphophobic, sexual or aggressive contents;

- Unusual perceptual experiences including somato-sensory (bodily) or other illusions, depersonalization or derealization;

- Vague, circumstantial, metaphorical, over-elaborate or stereotyped thinking, manifested by odd speech or in other ways, without gross incoherence;

- Occasional transient quasi-psychotic episodes with intense illusions, auditory or other hallucinations and delusion-like ideas, usually occurring without external provocation.

Another opinion was that he was suffering with schizophrenia. Mental Health America describes it this way:

Behaviors that are early warning signs of schizophrenia include

- Hearing or seeing something that isn't there
- A constant feeling of being watched
- Peculiar or nonsensical way of speaking or writing
- Strange body positioning
- Feeling indifferent to very important situations
- Deterioration of academic or work performance
- A change in personal hygiene and appearance
- A change in personality
- Increasing withdrawal from social situations
- Irrational, angry or fearful response to loved ones
- Inability to sleep or concentrate
- Inappropriate or bizarre behavior
- Extreme preoccupation with religion or the occult

You can see that both are very similar. The main difference I understand is that the schizophrenic person is not able to be convinced of the thinking errors they possess. With the schizotypal personality disorder, this is possible. I wholeheartedly believe this is the case with Johnathan based off my many encounters with him. Many times, he would say completely off the wall bizarre things and truly seem to believe them. But I was there, and I would say, "Okay, Johnathan. Let's really look at that." And I would talk to him about how the things he was saying or hearing or seeing were just not realistic. Nine times out of ten, he would think for a few minutes and then say, "Yeah. I can see what you mean. Yeah. You are right." And that usually settled the matter for him. If he had true schizophrenia, this would not have been the case.

The lady who labeled him with the tier level also believed him to have schizophrenia. She assigned him a tier level of 1, minimal risk to reoffend. This was his first time to offend, that is known, and therefore he was considered "nonviolent." Personally, if someone rapes someone, that is violent in my book. He assaulted me twice before, so, therefore, in my mind he *is* likely to reoffend. But welcome to the world of judicial gray areas.

After reading through the reports, I was incredibly angry all over again. Angry because the interviews that they all had with Johnathan quoted him as saying I had done a plethora of things contrary to my character and were completely off the charts. It made me sick to my stomach and left me in a state of shock. I cried a lot that night when I got home again. My healing scars were torn open, and my heart was seeping infection and blood. I wondered if this nightmare would *ever* be over.

Suzy contacted me to check up on me the next day. I told her of my frustration and hurt, and she gently reminded me that a jury of twelve people had agreed with me, believed me, and convicted him in a very short period of time. She also was optimistic regarding the overall reports because Johnathan could very clearly *not* use the mental disease or defect in sentencing, although she was sure the defense would try. It is also noteworthy to say that the State Mental Hospital did not find that he would benefit from treatment there and stated they would not want him there as a DPHH inmate. That knowledge helped. With all this being said, I did spend a considerable amount of time over the next few weeks healing from that whole experience. As it turned out, it was preparation for what was to come on sentencing day.

Leading up to this day, I was filled with the same old insecurities. I truly didn't know what to expect. I was filled with nervous anxiety about giving my victim impact statement. I wondered if Johnathan would start to spout off with crazy ramblings or if I would be able to get through my statement. I wondered if I would be able to do it without breaking down or if I would even be able to get through it at all. I wondered if the defense would have him cleaned up with his hair being cut and his face shaved or if he would still look like the maniac in his mug shot. The look on his face in that last photo was the same look I saw on his face that day when he violated me, and it sent chills down my spine each time I thought of it. Several people who had seen it said he looked a lot like Charles Manson. I must agree he did.

When we met with Suzy the last time before going into the courtroom, she told us the defense team's plan was to ask for twenty years suspended to the DPHH. She also had an educated guess that the psychologist they were calling was going to give an opinion on what sentencing should be. I hated the thought of seeing Satan's twin daughters again and hearing their insulting voices. I wondered if the jury members would come back to see what his fate would be. I wondered who all would be there to support us, and I wondered if he would actually have any family members show up to support him at all. I didn't have to wait long to find the answer to these questions.

We all walked together to the courtroom. Suzy said, "This is the last time you will have to make this journey to the courtroom, Barb. We are on the home stretch now. It's almost over." Over. I thought, "Oh, God, how I wished this all *were* over. I wished this had never happened." But it had, and so here we were. I was just moments away from the conclusion of the beginning of the end of this horrible chapter in my life.

When we arrived outside the courtroom, I was surprised and slightly shocked to see that Johnathan's brother, his sister-in-law, and his aunt were sitting in the courtroom. I had a sinking feeling in my gut that they were not there to be remotely supportive to me. It didn't take long before that reality was realized. The kids and us couldn't sit together, because the courtroom had already filled up. Al and I ended up sitting up front and the kids in the back. Except for a couple of official people, a journalist, and Johnathan's family, all who were present were there to support us. It was comforting. My counselor, Rob, showed up, even though I had not seen him since the end of December. Erin was there and greeted me with a giant hug of support. She sat behind me. Liz was there and was very emotional; the weight of the day was heavy on her heart. There were a lot of people there; the room was full.

As soon as I sat down, Johnathan began to stare at me intently. He was trying to intimidate me. He was alternating staring at me and then my husband, then back to me, then to Liz, and then back to me. No matter what I did to block his view, he moved so he could stare at me. So I started right back at him as if to say to him, "No. You are not going to scare me, and you are not going to intimidate me. It is over." When the stare down failed, he began to speak. He was complaining I brought my kids, and that he wouldn't be able to say anything because they were there and how I had lied about all of this. He vocally stated how I had done multiple things. He had an audience, so I guess he was going to use it.

The judge entered the room, and court was in session. Al started off with his victim impact statement. It was fierce and powerful, and the courtroom was silent as my husband told Johnathan he was a rapist at his core and would always be a rapist. He talked about me and our family and our marriage and our resolve to not let this ruin our family. Finally, he talked of forgiveness and offered it to Johnathan, but only after explaining to him that forgiveness does not mean reconciliation to us. He told him that he hoped he would find that in God, but if he didn't, it was on him.

Then it was my turn to speak. I stood a mere few feet away from Johnathan, and he was seated in shackles right in front of me. I read my entire victim impact statement, only stopping to put Johnathan in his place when he started to act up and protest. I am told I looked poised and gave my statement with dignity. I don't know. I was shaking from head to toe, even though I am told it didn't show. I looked him directly in the eyes multiple times, especially when I asked him where his shame, shock, or remorse were. It was a small victory for me just being able to stand there and speak my truth and be heard without dripping sarcasm from his defense attorneys and without interruption. I wanted the satisfaction of knowing he heard me loud and clear. And he did hear me, even though he squirmed a lot in his seat.

To Your Honor:

> In the matter of consideration for the sentencing of "Johnathan" for the crime he committed against me, "Attempted" Sexual Intercourse Without Consent, I would like to address you. I will first tell you about how much this has affected my life and changed me.
>
> To say I am a different person today than I was on October 12, 2015 is an understatement. I am no longer carefree and my world has been shattered. I am unable to participate in the same activities I once thrived at, such as my volunteerism with the homeless community. My heart has been changed. I no longer look at people with the same benefit of the doubt I used to give them. I doubt their motives and don't trust anyone in that sector of society. Many years ago when my husband and I were still just dating he made a comment about a person walking down the street. They were obviously homeless and down on their luck. My response to him was that they are probably a pretty nice person once you get to know them. And, I truly believed that to be true. Our family joke each time we went downtown for anything was, "Did you hug that one?" And the answer was usually yes. To have that part of my personality so completely slain is a shame and a loss to our community. People need people and I always was someone who would be there for anyone if they asked. Not so anymore. For my

own self-preservation and protection, that chapter of my book is closed.

This event has affected my family greatly. It has ripped my heart open to see my kids' faces during the time right after this occurred and for the months leading up to the trial. I hated to see my children cry when we told them what had happened. I hated to see my husband cry when he realized I had been hurt in this way and I hate that I can't do anything to erase any of it. It is now an ugly part of our new reality. The amount of heartache and stress from this has been insurmountable. I literally could not make it through one single day for months, maybe 6 or 7 straight months, without completely breaking down in a pile of tears, not just once but several times a day. Even now, I still find myself weeping nearly every day. For weeks my inability to sing was huge. I have always had a happy heart and singing has always been my joy. Although I have found my voice again, it was devastating to not be able to express my heart in that way. Music is my joy. He stole my joy when he did this to me.

Being attacked in this personal way from someone I knew so well and actually deeply cared for changed the way I view the world. For several months I was unable to even go into a grocery store without freaking out if anyone, especially a man came within 5 feet of my space. Just simply walking from the parking lot to the door and back was a great struggle where I needed to constantly remind myself that they were there for shopping just like me. The mental anguish I have suffered is deep. I took full advantage of any free counseling available to me until I exhausted that avenue. The SARC program at the U of M was a Godsend to me. I followed that up with YWCA and finally a professional counselor who I have seen twice a week for several months and then just once a week. 66 weeks of non-stop counseling, taking time away from my family for an hour and a half each week in the evening and leaving early from work to do so. Finally, I have been able to function without counseling since the beginning of January 2017. This is because I worked really hard to rebuild what was torn down. I believe if it were not for these resources I would not be here today to talk to you. The depth of grief I have born is without measure.

Our finances have suffered greatly as a result of this evil done to me. I have been unable to work as I have worked prior to this attack. I think it would be safe to say I have not been a very good employee since this happened. I am more impatient and unwilling to allow myself to be treated unkindly by others no matter what the reason. I have had to take many hours off to go to the courthouse and meet with the county attorney, or meet with the police, or meet with a counselor. None of these lost wages have been restored to me. Thankfully the state has provided me with the professional counseling I needed through the Crime Victim Advocate program or this would be an even greater loss to us. The physical damage done to my body by this man healed in approximately 10 days. But the residuals live on. If I may, I have prepared a statement to Johnathan and will include it here:

Hello, My Name Is Jane Doe. You stole my identity.

You stole my peace. You opened the floodgates of my eyes and burst the dam. You tried to crush my spirit. You stole what wasn't yours to take. You disregarded me as a human being. You closed your ears to my pleas. You repaid my selflessness with your selfishness. You mocked me for my faith. You drug my name through the mud and slung dirt at my face.

All the while pretending you didn't do this. I have wondered over and over again, "How? Why?" How could you, the person I freely gave my friendship to, turn around and rape me? Don't sit there and pretend you don't know right from wrong. How dare you play the part of the confused innocent man! You know what you did and you know you planned it. And you also know I know that about you too. You sized me up that day. You squeezed my injured foot and saw how much pain that caused me. You knew I was serious when I told you I would never come back to McCormick Park again since you were obviously living there again.

You hurt my body. Yes, it took a couple days for the full impact to hit me, but I assure you it did. You hurt my soul. You carelessly did what you did and then simply stepped back and put your hands down at your sides and looked at me with no expression. How black your soul must be to do that to the one person who believed in you and your potential. My body has healed from what you did that day. No more bruises and no more abrasions exist on my private parts. But the effects linger. The stress you have caused me has reared its ugly head in many ways. I am now 30+ pounds heavier. The stress hormone is present on my midsection like a lingering hangover. My digestive track is all messed up. I have heartburn like never before, my migraines last for weeks at a time, I am nauseous more often than not, I have body tremors and the fibromyalgia I have suffered with for years is now completely off the charts. I wake up each morning to a body that screams in agony. My every joint aches. My legs cramp and my shoulders throb from tension. I have no balance in my body anymore. It will take me months if not years to regain what you stole from me.

Nights are the worst for me. I don't sleep uninterrupted anymore. I wake up at 2:30, 3:30, 4:30, 5:30 and rarely sleep a whole night through, even with the aid of melatonin. I wake from nightmares and find myself in terror because I can't get myself regulated back to reality. My nightmares consist of you and that day. I feel your breath on my face, I feel the impact of your methodical and hard thrusting on me, I feel the sickness of the release you had on me, I smell your stench and I feel the total lack of my ability to do anything to stop you. I see the three people on the walking path walking by and I call out to them in my mind and yet they keep on moving.

When I look in the mirror I wonder who that is looking back at me. Because, I don't recognize that woman. She has a haunted expression in those eyes. You dimmed the brightness she once had in her eyes. She doesn't smile and laugh freely anymore. She is guarded and has deep sadness in her heart. She is a shadow of someone I once knew. Do you remember that person? I do. She was happy and bubbly and loving. She was full of kindness and compassion. She always gave the benefit of the doubt to everyone. She gave of herself freely and unreserved. That's what others say she was like. Not so anymore, thanks to you. How's your tummy feeling right now, Johnathan?

Jane exists because you stole my name. She is a faceless woman who lives with deep pain. She lost her song for weeks, not daring to utter anything but sobs. Hello, I am Jane Doe. I spent the first 3 months crying so much that the skin under my eyes was raw. I never used to have bags under my eyes, but I sure do now. I struggled every day just to get out of bed and go through each day as if nothing had happened. I despised each breath I took because that meant I was still here to live with the memories of what you did to me that day. I hold my breath when I cross over Orange Street Bridge. I don't dare to look in the direction of McCormick Park. I panic when I see a man in a red coat; even more so when they have long hair or a beard.

When I smell body odor it causes me to relive your nasty stench. The sensory overload is more than I can handle. My heart beats erratically, my palms sweat, my brain goes numb, my breathing is shallow, my legs go weak and I shake. I have to focus really hard and pep talk myself that I am ok and it isn't happening again, right here and right now. You stole my security. You stole my freedom. The things I once enjoyed are now a distant memory. I'm too full of anxiety to go out alone and walk or run. I don't even go to a park alone anymore to have my lunch. If I do go to a park, I sit inside my car with the windows up and the doors locked. On occasion if I get the courage to venture out of my car, my new best friend Mace is right there with me holding my hand. I can't relax. My body and mind are at full alert and I am extremely jumpy.

For 11 months, my "normal" was a big black cloud of uncertainty hanging over my head and the heads of my husband, son and daughter. How awful it is to know that as your victim I was going to be re-victimized by the system that was supposed to protect me from you, but instead protected you! Was it not enough to be violated by you on that day that you needed to put me and my family through more? You didn't even have the moral fiber in you to stand up like a man and admit what you did to me. Again, I have asked over and over, "Why? How?" Now I will ask you again, how does your tummy feel Johnathan? Where is your shock? Where is your remorse? Where is an inkling of sorrow for what you have done to me? Do you remember me now? Who am I? I am taking me back from you. You don't get to have that control and power over me anymore. I am picking up the shattered pieces of me and I am being glued back together again. And that light in my eyes that you attempted to block out with your hand? It's coming back. And it is brighter than ever. Why? Because I know the one who put that light there and he has never left me for a second. You will never be able to extinguish it. Was the light in me too bright for your darkness? Is that why you covered my eyes?

Today, Jane Doe will take her rest. She has served me well. She has protected me and given me time to face you. She has given me strength to be me. And I am proud to be me, despite what you did to me. This is your shame, not mine. Your actions have held me hostage for a long time. My hatred of you for what you did to me has held me hostage for a long time. But you don't get the luxury of that control any longer. I am releasing the anger and releasing the hatred and replacing it with things that have zero to do with you and your existence. Forgiveness is something I am working on. It is a choice I need to make every day of my life. I never thought you would hear the words "I forgive you" coming from me, but I do forgive you Johnathan. Not for your benefit, but mine. My faith dictates to me that I need to forgive you and because I do love God from the bottom of my heart, I will forgive you. I pray for this ability constantly and I even pray for you to be forgiven by God himself, but that is totally in your control, not mine. You are the one who needs to make that step toward him. Not me. My forgiveness to you, however, does not give you permission to vandalize my life in any way at any time and it does not release you of the reality of what you carried out on me. It simply sets me free. Free from anger and bitterness so I can continue to heal and become a better me.

Your new reality will soon begin. I hope you spend every single moment of your existence remembering the choices you made and I hope they are the cause of your own sleepless nights. I wish they would lock you up for the rest of your life and throw away the key. At least there you can't hurt me or anyone else again. And maybe, just maybe, you might finally get the help you need. You can't make it up to me and my family by saying you are sorry. You can't undo what you've done to me. You can't erase my nightmares and flashbacks. You can't make me who I once was. You have in effect given me a life sentence. I will live with the memories of your actions until the day I die. But my life will never be the unproductive excuse that you have chosen. And you did choose your path Johnathan. You have pushed away all who love you and tried to help you and you threw your life away by your own choice. Your mental illness is only a crutch for bad choices and bad behavior. Denial is a one way river and you hold the paddles. You still possess the ability to know right from wrong and to choose one or the other. You and I both know that. My life will be full and rich despite you. Because mine is full of love and goodness and grace and mercy. I will take this experience and learn from it and I will help others so they don't suffer as I have. Hello. My name is no longer Jane Doe. Rest in peace Jane. Hello. My name is strength. Hello. My name is dignity. Hello. My name is courage. Hello. My name is Barb Jenkins and you did not succeed in destroying me.

Your honor, I wish to thank you for allowing me the avenue to say what I needed to say here. I hope that in your consideration of the sentence you impart to Johnathan that his outburst at the end of the trial as the jury was leaving was not lost on you. I hope that you consider the look of utter evil that came upon his face and the body language that was so clearly evident as he contemplated what he would do to me if he was not under lock and key. I live with fear of the future. I ask you to please assure me that he is kept out of society for a very long time. For my protection and my family's protection and the protection of any other woman who would endeavor to show him kindness, please keep him away for as long as you can. I know that the maximum sentence is 100 years. I know the maximum sentence for him is probably unrealistic, but please consider that if I were to live another 100 years, his actions to me will never be undone. My sentence is for the rest of my life. All I am asking is that his is not merely a slap on the hand in effect bringing another slap to my face and the faces of all who are victimized in this way. Thank you for your time.

Respectfully,

Barb Jenkins

After I was done speaking, the defense team put on their show. The state had only called Al and me and didn't feel they needed to put on a show, since the reports and the recommendation from the Parole and Sentencing Review sided with us stating they felt forty years with twenty suspended would be appropriate. Defense, however, felt they needed to have a big show for Johnathan's sake. They started off by calling the psychologist who evaluated Johnathan while he was incarcerated in Missoula County Jail.

The defense couldn't really use the mental disease or defect in sentencing to get Johnathan off from serving time. Even so, they tried to do it anyway. The next three hours was spent listening to testimony about how Johnathan suffered with severe mental illness, and although they acknowledged he was not a viable candidate for treatment, he should be released into the public on probation for twenty years. They spent considerable time defaming me as much as they could. They referred to me as the "alleged victim" again, even though Johnathan had been tried and found guilty. All the while, Johnathan was spouting off and interjecting the whole time. It was so frustrating to me. I just wanted out of the courtroom. I was feeling like I was going to throw up, so I got up and left the courtroom. Shortly afterward, Liz came out and sat with me while Al went back in. Soon, my friend Jen came out and sat with us; next Rob came out, and so did Detective Franke and Erin. Everyone was just stunned by the mini-trial and the continued efforts to assassinate me and make everyone believe I had a voluntary sexual relationship with Johnathan. I was furious and disgusted and out of patience.

Finally, the judge addressed Johnathan and asked him if he had anything to say about what her sentence to him should be. He said he thought she should throw this out and reverse the conviction and make it all go away. She told him she was not going to do that. She reminded him he had been convicted by a jury of twelve of his peers, and she would not throw this out. Then Johnathan rambled on for a long time about how he was not mentally ill, not homeless for the last thirty years, had held a job, and was productive the whole time, how he had never had a mental break from using drugs and how I had given myself the injuries on my genitalia from masturbating in the shower. He said my husband came into the bathroom and found me masturbating, got jealous, and insisted I go to First Step to do the examination I had.

The only thing about the time he was speaking that was remotely satisfying to me was the looks on the faces of his defense attorneys and the lady who gave him the tier level. She had spent considerable time talking about how she would personally work with Johnathan in the local community upon his release that day. She sat in her seat, rolling her eyes and wringing her hands in desperation. One of his defense attorneys said under her breath, "You are not helping yourself." But the mic picked it up. The other wrote a note and slapped it down in front of him. I can surmise it said, "Shut up and sit down." But he just kept talking.

Finally, the judge looked at Johnathan again and said, "I need to know if there is anything you want me to consider before I sentence you." Johnathan looked at her and said, "Well, I *am* glad that she said she forgives me." The judge leaned in toward Johnathan and asked him, "Why? Is there some reason you would be glad that she forgives you? Is there something you need to be forgiven for?" Johnathan got a look on his face of panic and stood there for a bit before answering, "Nah." He waved it off with his hand. The judge tried again, "Well, if you are glad that she said she forgives you, why would you feel glad that she said that then?" He stood for a while again and then answered, "Uh, I'm just sorry that this has taken up so much of people's time." Upon hearing that, the judge asked both sets of counsels if there was anything further. "No, Your Honor."

Sentencing was prompt at that point. She told Johnathan he would be sentenced to the Department of Corrections in Deer Lodge MT for forty years with twenty suspended and a bunch of parole stipulations. When she pronounced his sentence, the bailiff took Johnathan out of the courtroom, and he had to pass right in front of me. This time, he didn't bother to stare at me, and he was finally silent as the weight of his sentence fell on him. The courtroom was cleared quickly. In the foyer, I was swamped with all those who were there to support me. We hugged, cried, and breathed a huge sigh of relief. This was over. I had stood up to my attacker and saw it through to the end, and it was finally over. I could now begin to *really* heal. I could put the ordeal in its respective place in the past of horrible memories and go home and lick my wounds.

"Are you happy?" Oh, what a weighty question. One would think I would be ecstatic, but the truth is that I would not classify the emotions I had running through me as happy. Relieved, yes. Exonerated, yes. Vindicated, yes. Mentally, physically, and spiritually exhausted, yes. I had so many emotions flooding me. I was unresponsive, and my face didn't really register anything, let alone happiness. I was not disappointed either, though. I was just overwhelmed, and I truly didn't know what to think or how to act or respond. It was weird. I had existed for the past year and a half in trauma mode, driven in large part on adrenaline to survive. Now it was time to switch gears, calm down, and really begin to heal. And, yes, there is an element of sadness that his life has gone so completely out of control. That said, I refuse to own that. It was by his own choice. While others have said they hope he is beaten and raped in prison, I actually do not wish that. I am not a cruel person. What I do wish is that he would someday acknowledge what he did and, thereby doing, start the journey toward his own healing and reconciliation to Jesus. As long as Johnathan continues to deny his crime, he can't find the spiritual freedom he needs.

While standing out in the foyer outside the courtroom, Johnathan's defense team walked by angrily. His family slipped away quickly and didn't say a word to me, much less look in my direction. I know that they had a lot to come to grips with knowing that Johnathan would soon be heading to prison for his vile crime against me. I didn't hold it against them. They did the best they could, despite what he did to me. I felt sorry for them more than anything. I am sure it had to have been hard to hear me and Al as we spoke the truth of our pain to Johnathan with our victim impact statements. But I think that our words and our pain had to be swirling around inside their heads, nestling into their hearts as they tried to wrap their brains around the fact that Johnathan had indeed raped me, and he would in fact be headed to prison for a long time to come. No matter how hard any of us try to make it make sense, it doesn't change the facts and the ugly truth. No amount of denial or victim blaming changes the fact that Johnathan carried out this evil act intentionally on me.

I watched the news and papers to see if news of Johnathan's sentence would be recorded. One of the odd things after the original press coverage is that the trial was not covered and the conviction had not even been mentioned in passing. Sentencing slipped by, and my powerful victim impact statement was heard only by those in the courtroom. That is with exception to an intern for the Missoulian from the University of Montana journalism studies. She had reached out to me after the trial and interviewed me. She followed my progress and attended the sentencing herself.

The next day, sitting in my office, she recanted how horrified she was by the actions of Johnathan's defense team and how insensitive and rude they were when I was reading my statement. I told her I truly wasn't paying attention to them. My focus was on Johnathan and making sure I had the chance to speak what I needed to speak. I wanted to make sure he heard me, so their antics were lost on me. Lucy Tompkins wrote an incredible article about my story, encapsulating the essence of what I was unable to verbalize over the last year and a half while going through the judicial system process. It was her first article published for the Missoulian, and it landed on the front page! It was entitled "Jane Doe: Missoula Woman's Ordeal after Sexual Assault."

After her article was published, I started receiving texts and messages on Facebook from many different people. Some I knew and many I did not know. All were positive, saying thank you for my bravery in speaking out and sharing my story, even letting my name be published. I gave a voice to the voiceless via Lucy's amazing accounting of my whole ordeal. Romans 8:28 was being lived out in amazing ways already. People were finding strength and courage to tell their own stories and begin to heal. If it helps *one* person, that is a victory in itself.

And so here I am now. My life has begun to settle into a more peaceful existence. I no longer have the questions and dread hanging over my head. The knots in my stomach are simmering down. My migraines are tapering off. My stress levels are evening out. I can breathe in and relax in the knowledge and assurance that Johnathan is not going to be allowed to roam in this community any time soon. Johnathan's fate is his own, and I do not spend my energy worrying about him or what may or may not happen with him. I can breathe. The jury that convicted Johnathan, the awesome police detective Bob Franke, along with the more-than-competent and incredibly caring county attorneys Suzy Boylan and Brian Lowney, my advocate Erin Shreder, and finally but certainly not the least, the Honorable Judge Karen Townsend have been used by the Lord to give me the best gift ever . . . peace and time. I can never thank them enough.

The tenth and final promise for this journey you've walked with me: "And surely I am with you always, to the very end of the age" (Matthew 28:20). Even though this verse is part of the great commission and is about an entirely different subject, the sentiment and reality of the words of Jesus are clearly the same. I am with you always. He was there with me in the day center when Johnathan walked in the door. He was with me on the many occasions I had spent time with Johnathan encouraging him to live a better life. He was with me when Johnathan raped me. He was with me in the aftermath. He is with me now. He has truly not left my side. He carried me when I couldn't carry myself. His strength and his reassurance have been present in every aspect, especially in the many facets of evil I have encountered since that day.

When Satan whispers in my ear that I am to blame, Jesus reminds me otherwise. When I feel the urge to marinate in the anger and betrayal, Jesus reminds me he is what I need to focus on. (Whatever is true, whatever is noble, whatever is pure ... think about such things.) When well-meaning people speak words that are judgmental, I am reminded they are ignorant from lack of experience dealing with trauma. When I am tempted to hang on to unforgiveness in my heart, I remember that I'm living in grace as a forgiven sinner too. I *must* forgive in order to be forgiven. One of the best things I've read is a quote that said, "Don't judge people just because they sin differently than you." For every negative hurtful thought, I have several in their place to remind me of my value in his eyes. It's a journey. This journey will only be laid to rest when I breathe my last breath on earth, and all this will be forgotten ... except that I have created this record to help educate and encourage others in my shoes. No pain, no sadness, no fear, no hate, no betrayal, no more demonic forces to break me. All will be made new. Oh, what a beautiful truth!

APPENDIX

———◆◆———

"Jane Doe: Who Is She?"

Statistics Source: RAINN (Rape, Abuse, Incest National Network) based on the annual National Crime Victimization Survey conducted by the US Justice Department

www.RAINN.org *Statistics vary with different researchers. The numbers range from 1 in every 3 to 1 in every 6 depending on where you read. The average is 1 in every 4 women according to current statistics as of June 2017. Not mentioned earlier but equally as important, 1 in 33 men are sexually assaulted. Also noteworthy is that male students are assaulted five times more than non-student males. 54 percent of all victims of rape and sexual assault are between the ages of 18–34.

Rape statistics

- When a person is raped in the United States, more than 90 percent of the time, the rapist gets away with it.
- Out of every 1,000 rapes, only 310 are reported to authorities.
- Fifty-seven (57) reports lead to arrests.
- Eleven (11) cases are referred to prosecutors.
- Seven (7) cases lead to a felony conviction.
- Six (6) rapists will be incarcerated.

Source: RAINN (Rape, Abuse and Incest National Network),

There are 1440 minutes in a day. My statistics are based off common math. 1440 minutes divided by 2 is 720 minutes each day that someone is assaulted. Take that times 7 and that is 5040 per week. Times that by 4 weeks per month and you have 20,160. Times that by 12 and you have 241,920 and I averaged up to an even

242,000. Since so many are unreported, it is near impossible to have an accurate count.

Population of US 325,146,000 taken from Wikipedia as of June 2017 This number varies slightly also depending on where you look. One source had our population over 326,425,000. http://worldometers.info http://worldpopulationreview.com/countries/united-states-population/

According to RAINN, 93 percent of women have PTSD related to rape/assault, 33 percent of women contemplate suicide after rape/assault, 13 percent attempt suicide after rape/assault.

Definition of *Trauma*
Webster: https://www.merriam-webster.com/dictionary/trauma
Definition of *PTSD*
Webster:
https://www.merriam-webster.com/dictionary/post-traumatic%20stress%20disorder

"The Wanderer: Where Am I?"
Definition of *Penetration*
US Legal: https://definitions.uslegal.com/s/sexual-penetration/

"You're So Strong"
Maranatha Singers—Abba Father http://maranathamusic.com/ http://decoda.com/the-maranatha-singers-abba-fatherwe-give-you-glory-lyrics

"The New You"
Definition of schizotypal personality disorder
Wikipedia: https://en.wikipedia.org/wiki/Schizotypal_personality_disorder
Definition of schizophrenia
Mental Health America:
http://www.mentalhealthamerica.net/conditions/schizophrenia#intro

ABOUT THE AUTHOR

———•◆•———

Barb Jenkins is a professional office manager and bookkeeper at a busy insurance agency in Missoula, Montana. She resides in Lolo, Montana, with her husband of twenty-eight years and their two children, Ethan and Grace. A native to Montana, she enjoys living in the mountains, hiking, and exploring outdoors; and she has a passion for music. Barb was born in Great Falls and has spent all but three years of her life in Montana. She was a shy and quiet child. Homelife was not easy for her growing up. She endured many forms of abuse from the start of her life until she left home at the age of eighteen. As a result of her upbringing, Barb struggled long and hard to find herself, trust in others, and break out of the low self-esteem she struggled with her whole life. Not growing up in an active Christian home, she still found God at an early age. This has been her firm foundation. She and her husband, Al, made a stable home life for themselves and their kids, living with Christ as the foundation. It is an absolute joy for her to be a mom and wife!

Barb found her niche in the Bible verse Hebrews 13:2: "Do not forget to show hospitality to strangers, for by so doing some have entertained angels unaware." She has spent her life dedicated to serving her family and others in the community and helping the less fortunate. She loves to organize events and especially ones that honor a particular group of people such as military, police, and the homeless. She finds great satisfaction in serving on the praise team at her church, Echo Missoula. Singing is a sign of a happy heart, and she is well-known for her faith, kindness, gentleness, smile, and big warm hugs. There is no such thing as strangers to Barb, only friends she hasn't met yet.

No stranger to adversity, Barb has deep faith convictions to carry her through. She wants nothing more than to encourage and guide others along a path of healing, hope, and restoration in the Lord. She loves with fierce love and is a loyal friend to everyone. Being a survivor of a brutal rape that took place in a public park and in broad daylight, she has had to fight hard through the mass of emotional, spiritual, physical, and legal pain of healing in a world where such things are barely talked about, and survivors are labeled guilty and less than. She is no longer a victim, no longer known as Jane Doe. Barb is a survivor and a warrior for those who have suffered the same injustice as she did at the hands of a rapist. In him, she is complete and more than a conqueror. She knows that he makes beauty out of ashes and is proud to be used as his mouthpiece.

CPSIA information can be obtained
at www.ICGtesting.com
Printed in the USA
FSHW010756090419
57067FS